The Art of

THE CHECKMATE

BY *Georges Renaud* AND *Victor Kahn*

CHAMPIONS OF FRANCE, 1923 AND 1934

Translated from the French by
W. J. TAYLOR

DOVER PUBLICATIONS, INC.
NEW YORK

International Standard Book Number
ISBN-13: 978-0-486-20106-1
ISBN-10: 0-486-20106-6

Manufactured in the United States by LSC Communications
20106621   2017
www.doverpublications.com

TABLE OF CONTENTS

Introduction

When a player, after examining a position carefully, has selected and played what seems to him the best move, it is very annoying to hear one of the onlookers remark:

"Everyone to his own taste. Personally, I should have announced mate in two."

The player is astonished and disappointed to realize that such is the case and that the too hasty exchanges he has made have deprived him of the chance of mating his opponent.

This is a typical position,

END-GAME NO. 1

Black to play

which occurred in a club tournament. It was Black's turn to play. He thought a while, lifted the Queen and triumphantly placed it on his Q6, threatening . . . Q–B7 mate.

White played RxB, giving back the exchange, and managed to exchange Queens a few moves later. He had two Pawns to the good, and won the game easily.

When the game was over, the loser said:

"There was nothing I could do. I had already sacrificed two Pawns and the exchange for an attack, which never came off."

Replacing the pieces in their original position, we showed him that there was a forced mate in two moves. The player looked carefully at the position and exclaimed:

"Well, I never . . . !"

He had discovered too late:

1. . . . Q–QB6 ch; 2. PxQ, B–R6 mate.

This is a classic mate discovered by Boden in 1857, and has occurred many times since. It is quite possible that the player we have just mentioned had come across it in a Chess book or magazine and had forgotten it because it had never been properly explained to him.

The first thing for the reader to learn is to see every possible mate; this is one of the requisites of a good player.

If one points out to a player a position in which there is a mate in five moves, he will find it in time; but let the same position occur in a game and the chances are eighty to a hundred he will be blind to the fact.

Even the greatest Chess masters have been no excep-

tion to the rule. Here are two very instructive examples:

In a match game Schiffers–Tchigorin (Berlin, 1897), the following position was reached:

Black played ... P–Kt3 and the game was drawn, whereas he might have announced mate in five moves.

1. ...	R–R8 ch !
2. KtxR	B–R7 ch !
3. KxB	R–R1 ch
4. K–Kt3	Kt–B4 ch
5. K plays	R–R5 mate.

At Hastings in 1938, the following position arose in a game Fairhurst–Reshevsky. Reshevsky thought a long while and played P–R3? He had overlooked a classic mate in seven moves.

END-GAME NO. 3

FAIRHURST   S. RESHEVSKY
Hastings, 1938

END-GAME NO. 2

Black mates in 5 moves

Black mates in 7 moves

1. . . .	R—B8 ch
2. BxR	Q—R2 ch
3. Q—Kt6	QxQ ch
4. R—Q4	QxR ch
5. K—R1	Kt—B7 ch
6. K—Kt1	Kt—R6 double ch
7. K plays	Q mate.

A number of these oversights can be detected in master play. In fact, certain Chess newspapers publish whole columns under the heading "Master Blunders." Such human failings should be encouraging to the average player.

But if great masters like Tchigorin and Reshevsky fail to see such mates because of time trouble, how much more likely it is in the case of the average player.

Moreover, these mates are the easiest combinations to be found over the board, for they consist of a series of checks with forced answers. Above all, these mates can be practically reduced to a few types with easily remembered characteristics.

It is necessary to know the typical mating positions for the following reasons:

1) To apply the mating maneuvers mechanically without loss of time when met with in games.

2) To try and obtain such positions when one has the initiative.

3) To avoid becoming a victim.

When a move is about to be played there is no guardian angel to whisper:

"Careful, friend. There is a forced mate in four moves; look out for it."

The aim of this book is to impart to you the information which will enable you to miss no opportunity of mating in typical positions.

Many Chess books quote a famous handicap game in which three Chess masters, Walker, Morphy and Steinitz, mated amateurs in exactly the same manner. Let us see how.

GAME NO. 1

Evans Gambit Accepted

New York, 1857

P. MORPHY   AMATEUR

(*Without the Queen's Rook*)

1.	P—K4	P—K4
2.	Kt—KB3	Kt—QB3
3.	B—B4	B—B4
4.	P—QKt4	BxP
5.	P—B3	B—R4
6.	P—Q4	PxP
7.	O—O	

A century ago this opening was played as automatically as the Queen's gambit declined is played nowadays.

7. . . .   Kt—B3 ?

Experience has taught us that in this position the only right move is 7. . . . B—Kt3.

8. B—R3   B—Kt3 ?

There is, even at this point, no satisfactory move. The only one which allows Black further resistance is 8. . . . P—Q3. From now on the game proceeds like clockwork.

9. Q—Kt3   P—Q4

Giving back the Pawn to parry the threat: 10. BxP mate.

10. KPxP   QKt—R4

With this simultaneous attack on White's Queen and Bishop, Black hopes to get rid of the dangerous Bishop.

11. R—K1 ch   B—K3

Starting a very pleasant combination. White, who is already playing minus a Rook, sacrifices his Queen.

12. PxB !   KtxQ

This sacrifice should have been declined, but in any case Black's position is hopeless.

White announces mate in 6 moves:

After Black's 11th move

13. PxP ch	K—Q2
14. B—K6 ch	K—B3
15. Kt—K5 ch	K—Kt4
16. B—B4 ch	K—R4
17. B—Kt4 ch	K—R5
18. PxKt mate.	

Is there an infallible recipe for such mates? We do not think so. In the example we have just given the King was collected at its initial square and gradually dragged to the other side of the board, where it was mated.

One thing can be said, however: An experienced player feels instinctively that positions, such as the one in the diagram, are full of latent possibilities. Since all the moves are forced and since there are no variations to complicate the line of play, it is relatively easy, with some practice, to foresee the consequences of the sacrifice and to calculate the number of moves necessary to bring about the mate. And even if he is not able to foresee the whole mating process, the good player will "feel" that the King is about to embark on a journey from which it will not come back.

Here is another famous game to which the same principles apply:

GAME NO. 2

Dutch Defense

London, 1912

EDWARD LASKER	SIR GEORGE A. THOMAS
1. P—Q4	P—K3
2. Kt—KB3	P—KB4
3. Kt—B3	Kt—KB3
4. B—Kt5	B—K2
5. BxKt	BxB
6. P—K4	PxP
7. KtxP	P—QKt3
8. Kt—K5	O—O
9. B—Q3	B—Kt2
10. Q—R5	

It is impossible to parry the threatening attack on Black's KR2. If *10. . . . P—KR3; 11. Q—Kt6* wins. And if *10. . . . P—Kt3; 11. KtxP, PxKt;*

12. QxP ch, B—Kt2; 13. Kt—Kt5 and wins.

10. . . .   Q—K2

After Black's 10th move

The text move seems to save the game, for Black's KR2 is covered by the Queen after 11. KtxB ch, PxKt. This position, however, is as full of hidden possibilities as the one in the Morphy game we have just quoted.

Edward Lasker announced mate in 8 moves.

11. QxP ch !!	KxQ
12. KtxB double ch	K—R3
13. Kt(5)—Kt4 ch !	K—Kt4
14. P—KR4 ch	K—B5
15. P—KKt3 ch	K—B6
16. B—K2 ch	K—Kt7
17. R—R2 ch	K—Kt8
18. K—Q2 mate.	

This death march of the King seems amazing to the

beginner. But, since all the moves are forced, the combination can be calculated accurately without a considerable mental effort. Here also, no definite rule can be laid down. The idea is to snatch the King from its initial square and by checking it constantly to lead it to the fatal mating square.

It is a question of rapid judgment, imagination and practice.

To be able to mate in a definite position, two conditions are required:

1) To be aware of a possible mate.

2) To be able to carry it out.

We have therefore endeavored to classify methodically all such positions; and for each one we have given the mating process. We then give three practical examples to illustrate each mate. The first includes games which end with the typical mate; the second includes games which end with a variation, or modification, of the typical mate. The third is rather more complicated. Between strong players it is rare that such typical mates occur. In most cases there is just the threat of a mate. In order to avoid it, the opponent is compelled to make a defensive move, which either weakens his position or results in loss of material.

In ninety-five games out of a hundred the two opponents castle; and ninety times out of a hundred they castle on the King's side. We shall therefore suppose, in the examples we are about to give, that all attacks are delivered against a castled position on the King's side. And if such an attack is to take place, certain preliminary conditions have to be fulfilled:

1) The castled position must show a weakness.

There are two kinds of weaknesses:

a) Permanent and irrevocable ones, such as the advance of one of the Pawns protecting the castled position (KBP, KKtP, KRP).

b) Temporary ones, such as the removal of Pieces which defend the castled position. For instance: the removal of the King's Knight or of one of the Pieces which protect the King's Knight; King's Bishop on K2; QKt on Q2; Queen on Q1.

2) The possibility of exploiting such a weakened position. For this it is necessary to have:

a) Open lines (files, ranks or diagonals) on the castled position of the opponent.

b) Pieces on these open lines.

c) More Pieces for the attack than the opponent has for the defense. It is immaterial whether the Defender's total number of Pieces is superior to the Attacker's; the important point is that these Pieces have neither the time nor the opportunity to reach the crucial defensive spot.

These are the principles which will constantly be used. They are equally applicable to positional and tactical play. In fact, they rule the conduct of the game.

Although the scope of this study is limited to typical mating positions, it will, we hope, initiate the reader gradually into the general methods of play. The best way to learn the principles of the game is to see their application in the most dramatic situation of the Chessboard: mate which can be announced in a definite number of moves.

Before we end this introduction let us remind the reader that, although these typical mating positions are met often, the mates do not always occur. In fact, they rarely occur with players of equal strength. One of them may resign because he has lost a Piece, or even a Pawn; or he may realize that the end-game is hopeless. Let the reader, therefore, not imagine that he will always be able to force a typical mate; or even think he may sacrifice Pieces at random. Each mate demands the fulfillment of certain conditions. And if one of the conditions is missing, the sacrifice is useless, and will simply leave the player with one or two Pieces down and a lost game.

Let us be bold by all means—it is the only way to victory!—but let us be cautious as well.

Part 1

PICTURESQUE MATES

In the first part of this book we shall study:
1) Legal's pseudo-sacrifice, and show how it is applicable to many positions.
2) The double check, for it is one of the fundamental elements of all mating attacks.
3) The smothered mate, which belongs in a class by itself.
4) The "Épaulettes" and "Guéridon" mates.
5) Greco's sacrifice.

This is an arbitrary classification. Except for Greco's mate, they are not typical mates in the true sense of the word. For this reason we shall give this first part a conventional denomination and call it "Picturesque Mates."

CHAPTER 1: *Legal's Pseudo-Sacrifice*

We have not called this chapter "Legal's Mate," but "Legal's Pseudo-Sacrifice," because it is rather more an attacking maneuver than an actual mate. In certain cases this maneuver leads to a mate, and in other cases to a decisive gain of material.

GAME NO. 3

Philidor Defense

Played in Paris, about 1750

KERMUR DE LEGAL   X.

De Kermur, Sire de Legal (1710–1792), was a strong French player, considered the champion of the Café de la Régence till he was beaten by A. D. Philidor, who was his pupil.

1.	P–K4	P–K4
2.	Kt–KB3	P–Q3
3.	B–B4	B–Kt5

Although this move looks strong, it is not always wise to pin the opponent's King's Knight at such an early stage of the game, for the following reasons:

1) Because the Bishop can be driven away with advantage (4. P–R3, B–R4), or else it can be compelled to take the Knight (4. P–R3, BxKt), thus speeding up White's development as the Queen comes into play.

2) It is always preferable to develop the Knights before the Bishops, because the latter have a much larger scope and can choose at their own convenience a square, depending on what line of play the opponent chooses.

After White's 5th move

3) Because a pin is only a relative pin when the Queen

is behind the Knight. As will be seen later, the Knight may move in spite of the pin, threatening Bishop, check, and, in certain cases, mate.

4. Kt—B3   P—KKt3 ?
5. KtxP !

This brilliant move was discovered by Legal.

5. . . . .   BxQ ? ? ?

A very bad blunder. Black instinctively grabs the Queen without noticing the threat. He thinks that he is just taking advantage of an oversight. The lesser evil was 5. . . . . PxKt; 6. QxB, and White has won a Pawn, with a considerable superiority of development. After the next move, White mates in two.

6. BxP ch   K—K2
7. Kt—Q5 mate.

Pattern of the Legal mate

Black is mated

The Typical Legal Mate

What is the use of studying this mate at length, the reader will wonder. It is two hundred years old, and quoted in every Chess book; all players know it by heart, and there is not the faintest ghost of a chance of ever using it in a game.

This objection is hardly valid. We do not ask you to learn this mate by heart. It is far more important to learn how it is brought about, and to realize the fact that the Queen's Bishop on Kt5 is unsupported and *en prise* if the King's Knight leaves his KB3 to threaten mate. This mating device occurs in many positions as a potential threat; and the opponent must take this into consideration if he intends to pin the King's Knight in the early stages of the game.

Even today many people are taken in by this famous two-hundred-year-old mate; and all strong players know they will have the opportunity to use it sometime in simultaneous displays. The victims themselves have heard of it and even know it by heart; but since the details of the position differ, and since they have never properly understood the mechanics of such a mate, they get trapped like beginners.

We now give you a few examples of this mate:

GAME NO. 4

Scotch Gambit

Vienna, 1847

E. FALKBEER   X.

E. Falkbeer (1819–1885) was a strong Austrian player and the inventor of the gambit which bears his name: 1. P–K4, P–K4; 2. P–KB4, P–Q4, etc.

1. P–K4   P–K4
2. Kt–KB3   Kt–QB3
3. P–Q4   PxP
4. B–B4

White gives up a Pawn to speed up his development.

4. . . .   P–Q3

Black shuts in his King's Bishop. Better would have been 4. . . . Kt–B3, developing a Piece.

5. P–QB3

Definitely giving up the idea of recapturing the Pawn (5. KtxP), as White chooses to bring as many Pieces as possible into action.

5. . . .   PxP
6. KtxP   B–Kt5

The bad pin!

7. O–O   Kt–K4

A presumptuous move. Black, who is already very backward in his development, thinks he can attack. The refutation is convincing and dramatic.

8. KtxKt

Winning at least a Piece, since Black's best answer is 8. . . . PxKt; 9. QxB.

8. . . .   BxQ?

Blind and greedy!

9. BxP ch   K–K2
10. Kt–Q5 mate.

GAME NO. 5

Vienna Game

Played March 16, 1900, at Hanover in a simultaneous blindfold exhibition against twelve players

H. N. PILLSBURY   FERNANDEZ

Harry Nelson Pillsbury (1872–1906) was the strongest American player of his time. He had a very aggressive style and won many prizes in international tournaments: first prize, Hastings (1895), second prize, Paris (1900), first prize, Munich (1900). He was also a remarkable blindfold player, and held the then world's record with twenty-three blindfold, simultaneous games. He invented a variation of the Queen's gambit declined, commonly known as the Cambridge Springs defense, and also an attacking position in the same gambit. He was Champion of the United States from 1897 until his death in 1906.

1. P—K4	P—K4
2. Kt—QB3	Kt—QB3
3. P—KB4	P—Q3
4. Kt—B3	P—QR3 ?

A lost tempo!

| 5. B—B4 | B—Kt5 |

The same absurd pin!

| 6. PxP | KtxP ? |

As in the previous game, Black has the same misplaced ambition of wanting to attack his opponent, with an undeveloped position.

7. KtxKt !	BxQ ??
8. BxP ch	K—K2
9. Kt—Q5 mate.	

GAME NO. 6

Danish Gambit

Great Britain, 1912

A. G. ESSERY   F. H. WARREN

Both players are British amateurs.

1. P—K4	P—K4
2. P—Q4	PxP
3. P—QB3	PxP
4. B—B4	P—Q3
5. KtxP	Kt—KB3
6. Kt—B3	B—Kt5

Wherever Chess is played this pin seems to fascinate players.

| 7. O—O | Kt—B3 |
| 8. B—KKt5 | |

White foresees the coming blunder and pins the King's Knight.

8. . . .	Kt—K4
9. KtxKt	BxQ
10. BxP ch	K—K2
11. Kt—Q5 mate.	

GAME NO. 7

Italian Opening

Played in 1929 at Leysin (Switzerland) in a simultaneous exhibition

A. CHÉRON   X.

André Chéron, born in Colombes, 1895, has been Champion of France three times (1926, 1927 and 1929). He is author of the *Traité complet d'Échecs* (*Complete Treatise on Chess*). André Chéron specialized at first in the didactic study of the end-game, and later he published a systematic essay on the end-game of Rook and Pawn against Rook.

He is also a well-known and successful problem composer whose specialty has been the strategical problem, made popular in France by G. Renaud. His theory on this type of problem, *Les Échecs Artistiques* (*Artistic Chess*), is a model of logic and coherence.

1. P—K4	P—K4
2. Kt—KB3	Kt—QB3
3. B—B4	P—Q3
4. Kt—B3	B—Kt5
5. P—KR3	B—R4 ?

The right move to avoid any trouble is: 5. . . . BxKt.

6. KtxP !	BxQ ?

The lesser evil is 6. . . . KtxKt; 7. QxB, KtxB; 8. Q—QKt5 ch, followed by 9. QxKt, with a better game and an extra Pawn.

7. BxP ch	K—K2
8. Kt—Q5 mate.	

The Second Aspect of the Legal Mate

If K2 is already obstructed (usually by a Bishop), the Legal sacrifice is possible without the co-operation of the Queen's Knight. Let us start with a typical example specially made up to illustrate this second aspect of the Legal mate.

GAME NO. 8

Alapin Opening

1. P—K4	P—K4
2. Kt—K2	

This is an obsolete opening. A move which shuts in two Pieces cannot be recommended.

2. . . .	Kt—KB3
3. P—Q3	B—B4
4. B—Kt5 ?	KtxP !

5. BxQ ? ?	BxP mate.

White is mated

There are numerous examples of the Legal mate which happen in this way, but not always as simply as in the game we have just quoted. Here are a few other examples:

GAME NO. 9

Italian Opening

Germany, 1837

B. HORWITZ   L. BLEDOW

1.	P—K4	P—K4
2.	Kt—KB3	Kt—QB3
3.	B—B4	B—B4
4.	P—B3	B—Kt3
5.	P—Q4	Q—K2
6.	P—Q5	Kt—Q1
7.	B—K2	P—Q3
8.	P—KR3 ?	P—KB4
9.	B—KKt5	Kt—B3
10.	QKt—Q2	O—O
11.	Kt—R4	PxP
12.	KtxP	KtxKt

The Legal sacrifice. White falls blindly into the trap. And don't suppose that B. Horwitz was a poor player. He was born in Mecklenburg (1807) and lived in London, where he co-operated with J. Kling on the world-famous book on end-games, *Chess studies* (1851).

Ludwig Bledow was a strong German player, who invented the counter-gambit which bears his name.

This happened, however, in 1837—and the Legal sacrifice was only a hundred years old!

13.	BxQ	BxP ch
14.	K—B1	Kt—Kt6 mate.

This mating combination

was made possible by White's eighth move.

GAME NO. 10

Philidor Defense

Played in 1852

C. F. SMITH   X.

(*Without the Queen's Knight*)

1.	P—K4	P—K4
2.	Kt—KB3	P—Q3
3.	B—B4	P—QB3
4.	P—Q4	B—K3 ?
5.	B—KKt5	Q—Q2 ?
6.	Q—K2	B—Kt5 ?
7.	PxP	PxP
8.	R—Q1	Q—B2
9.	KtxP !	BxQ ?
10.	R—Q8 ch	QxR
11.	BxP mate.	

GAME NO. 11

Ruy Lopez

Graz (Austria), 1888

J. BERGER   FRÖLICH

Johann Berger, born in Graz (1845–1934), was a strong player who always distinguished himself in international tournaments and was also a gifted problem composer. He published many Chess studies and a book on end-games, *Theorie und Praxis der Endspiele* (Leipzig, 1890), which is still read the world over.

1.	P—K4	P—K4
2.	Kt—QB3	Kt—QB3
3.	Kt—B3	P—Q3
4.	B—Kt5	B—Kt5 ?

5. Kt–Q5	Kt–K2
6. P–B3	P–QR3
7. B–R4	P–QKt4
8. B–Kt3	Kt–R4

Black should get ready to castle on the King's side instead of starting useless maneuvers on the Queen's wing.

9. KtxKP !	BxQ ?

Notice the following pleasant variation: 9. . . . KtxB; 10. KtxB, KtxR; 11. KKt–B6 ch !, PxKt; 12. KtxKBP mate.

With a better defense, Black loses a Pawn. 9. . . . KtxB; 10. KtxB, KtxKt; 11. PxKt, etc.

10. Kt–KB6 ch	PxKt
11. BxP mate.	

GAME NO. 12

Four Knights' Opening
Played in 1890

POLLOCK   HALL

1. P–K4	P–K4
2. Kt–KB3	Kt–QB3
3. Kt–B3	B–Kt5
4. B–B4	Kt–B3
5. O–O	P–Q3
6. Kt–Q5	B–Kt5
7. P–B3	KB–B4
8. P–Q3	Kt–K2

This position is similar to the one of the previous game.

9. KtxP !	BxQ ?
10. KtxKt ch	PxKt

If instead 10. . . . K–B1; 11. KKt–Q7 ch, QxKt; 12. KtxQ ch, K–K1; 13. KtxB, followed by 14. RxB, and White is a Piece and Pawn up.

11. BxP ch	K–B1
12. B–R6 mate.	

GAME NO. 12A

Philidor Defense
Played in New York, 1868

G. H. MACKENZIE   F. PERRIN

G. H. Mackenzie was born in Bellfield (Scotland) in 1837 and died in New York in 1891. He became an American citizen in 1858 and was very successful in international tournaments from 1870 to 1890. He won the first prize in 1887 at Frankfurt ahead of Blackburne, S. Bardeleben, S. Tarrasch and J. Berger.

F. Perrin was an American player, especially known for the games he lost against Morphy.

1. P–K4	P–K4
2. Kt–KB3	P–Q3
3. P–Q4	P–KB3 ?
4. B–QB4	Q–K2 ?
5. O–O	Kt–B3
6. Kt–B3	B–Kt5
7. Kt–Q5	Q–Q1
8. P–B3	KKt–K2
9. PxP	KtxP
10. KtxKt !	BxQ
11. KtxKBP ch	PxKt
12. B–B7 mate.	

Third Aspect of the Legal Mate

The King's Knight is essential for the defense of the castled position, and also of the King, if the castling has not yet taken place.

Its removal or exchange enables the opponent, in certain cases, to employ the Legal sacrifice, with the aid of his Queen's Bishop.

GAME NO. 13

Kieseritzky–Boden Gambit

TAYLOR   X.

1.	P–K4	P–K4
2.	B–B4	Kt–KB3
3.	Kt–KB3	KtxP
4.	Kt–B3	KtxKt
5.	QPxKt	P–Q3 ?

This is a losing move; it could have been immediately refuted by 6. Kt–Kt5 !

6.	O–O	B–Kt5 ?
7.	KtxP !	BxQ ?
8.	BxP ch	K–K2
9.	B–Kt5 mate.	

Black is mated

The same thing may easily happen to White as the next game will show.

GAME NO. 14

Petroff's Defense

(MADE-UP VARIATION)

1.	P–K4	P–K4
2.	Kt–KB3	Kt–KB3
3.	KtxP	Kt–B3

Black could have easily recaptured the Pawn (3. . . . . P–Q3 and 4. . . . KtxP). The next move allows White to keep the Pawn, but at the expense of his development.

4. KtxKt   QPxKt

White has time enough to defend his KP, but as a compensation for the sacrificed Pawn, Black has already three minor Pieces in action, whereas White has only one.

5.	P–Q3	KB–B4
6.	B–Kt5	KtxP !

This brilliant sacrifice leaves White quite defenseless. For instance: 7. PxKt, BxP ch; 8. K–K2, B–Kt5 ch; 9. KxB, QxQ, and wins. Or else: 7. Q–K2, BxP ch; 8. K–Q1, QxB; 9. QxKt ch, and Black may either play B–K3 (with an extra Pawn and the better development), or K–Q1, with crushing threats. Finally: 7. B–K3 (sad retreat!), BxB; 8. PxB, Q–R5 ch; 9. P–KKt3, KtxKtP; 10. PxKt (forced), QxR.

| 7. BxQ | BxP ch |
| 8. K–K2 | B–Kt5 mate. |

GAME NO. 15

King's Gambit Declined

Played in Paris, February 5, 1887, *in a simultaneous exhibition*

J. TAUBENHAUS   COLCHESTER

Jean Taubenhaus (1850–1920) was born in Warsaw and settled in Paris in 1883. He was a second-rate master, whose best achievement was the London tournament of 1886, where he placed third, after Blackburne and Burn. He gave lessons at the Café de la Régence, where he used to play every day. He is the author of *Traité du Jeu d'Échecs*, published in 1910.

1. P–K4	P–K4
2. P–KB4	P–Q3
3. Kt–KB3	B–Kt5
4. B–B4	Kt–KB3
5. PxP	KtxP
6. Kt–B3	KtxKt
7. QPxKt	Kt–B3
8. O–O	KtxP(K4)
9. KtxKt !	BxQ ?
10. BxP ch	K–K2
11. B–KKt5 mate.	

The Fourth Aspect of the Legal Mate

The Legal sacrifice does not necessarily lead to mate in three or four moves. Whether accepted or declined, it may simply give a decisive advantage.

Here is a game that has been played a number of times and published in many Chess books. It has been attributed to J. Mieses as well as to J. Préti, but is probably much older. The attacking player recaptures the Queen with profit, thanks to a discovered check.

GAME NO. 16

Center Counter-Gambit

Nuremberg Tournament, 1895

J. MIESES   J. OEHQUIST

J. Mieses, born in Leipzig (1865), is the oldest living international master, and holds a long record of brilliancy prizes in international tournaments, though without ever attaining first place.

J. Oehquist was a Scandinavian player.

    1. P—K4   P—Q4

A violent attempt to control the center.

    2. PxP   QxP
    3. Kt—QB3

This proves in a most convincing manner how rash it is to play the Queen in the early stages of the game, as White is able to develop a Piece with the gain of a tempo.

    3. . . .   Q—Q1
    4. P—Q4   Kt—QB3

A weak move. Instead of attacking the Queen's Pawn, Black should develop his King's side Pieces, preparatory to castling.

    5. Kt—KB3   B—Kt5

Pinning the Knight and threatening to win the Queen's Pawn.

    6. P—Q5   Kt—K4

A fatal move!

    7. KtxKt   BxQ

The greediness does not pay! White not only takes back the Queen—he also wins the game.

    8. B—Kt5 ch   P—B3
    9. PxP   resigns.

Black loses

It is easy to see that Black must lose, whatever defense he chooses. Here is an example: 9. . . . Q—B2; 10. PxP ch, K—Q1; 11. KtxP mate. The reader will be able to see for himself what happens after 9. . . . Q—Kt3, or 9. . . . P—QR3.

In the next example it will be interesting to see how the Legal sacrifice may be employed in one of the well-known opening variations of the Queen's gambit declined, which most players play almost mechanically.

GAME NO. 17

Queen's Gambit Declined

(OPENING VARIATION)

1. P—Q4	P—Q4
2. P—QB4	P—K3
3. Kt—QB3	Kt—KB3
4. B—Kt5	QKt—Q2

This position is met hundreds of times. White must not attempt to win a Pawn, taking advantage of the pin; if he does, this is what happens:

5. PxP	PxP
6. KtxP ??	KtxKt !
7. BxQ	B—Kt5 ch
8. Q—Q2	

The only move.

| 8. . . . | BxQ |
| 9. KxB | KxB |

And Black has won a Knight.

After White's 6th move

CHAPTER 2: The Power of the Double Check

A check may be parried either by moving the King, by capturing the checking Piece, or by interposing something between the King and the checking Piece, provided the latter is not a Knight. A double check, on the other hand, can only be parried by moving the King. Both Pieces giving the double check may be *en prise* without decreasing the force of the attack.

All players know that the consequences of a double check may often prove fatal; and for this reason they must be careful to avoid them.

What is less known is the fact that the double check, by compelling the King to move, may draw it into a mating net. This may often occur at the very beginning of the game.

Our first game is an elementary but typical example of how the King is mated on its initial square in the early part of the game.

GAME NO. 18

King's Gambit

U. S. A., about 1859

A. B. MEEK   X.

A. B. Meek, an American player born in Alabama, was a contemporary of Morphy, and took part in the New York tournament of 1857.

1. P—K4	P—K4
2. P—KB4	PxP
3. Kt—KB3	P—Q4

A typical counterattack.

4. Kt—B3	PxP
5. KtxP	QB—Kt5
6. Q—K2	

Threatening a double check.

6. . . .   BxKt ?

Better would have been 6. . . . B—K2

7. Kt—B6 double ch
     and mate.

Note how both mating Pieces are *en prise*. Of course,

Black is mated

it needed a tremendous blunder for such a mate to take place. In practice it seldom happens, the double check being used mainly as a threat.

We shall now give an opening variation of the "Giuoco Piano," showing one of the ways a double check may be used.

GAME NO. 19

Giuoco Piano

(OPENING VARIATION)

1. P—K4	P—K4
2. Kt—KB3	Kt—QB3
3. B—B4	B—B4
4. P—Q3	KKt—K2

A mistake. The normal place for the King's Knight is KB3, where it prevents White from playing Q—R5. White takes immediate advantage of this error.

5. Kt—Kt5

Attacking the KBP a second time.

5. . . .	O—O
6. Q—R5	

Threatening mate and attacking the KBP for the third time. This proves convincingly how incautious Black's fourth move was, since he cannot stop the mate and protect the KBP simultaneously.

6. . . .	P—KR3

There is no other move.

7. KtxP

Threatening the Queen. Black should sacrifice the exchange (7. . . . RxKt), although his game would still be hopeless. But Black chooses a quicker end:

7. . . .	Q—K1
8. KtxRP double ch	K—R2
9. Kt—B7 ch	K—Kt1
10. Q—R8 mate.	

The Preparatory Sacrifice

In order to lure the King into a position where it can receive a double check, resulting in a mating attack or a decisive gain of material, one should not hesitate to sacrifice a Piece, even the Queen.

In the following game we shall show how a Bishop was sacrificed to achieve this result.

GAME NO. 20

Scotch Gambit

Germany, about 1885

A. FRITZ   X.

After Black's 7th move

1.	P—K4	P—K4
2.	Kt—KB3	Kt—QB3
3.	P—Q4	KtxP

The usual move is 3. . . . . PxP.

4.	KtxP	Kt—K3
5.	B—B4	P—KB3 ?

In an open game this move should be avoided, because it opens the dangerous diagonal R5—K8 to the White Queen.

6.	Q—R5 ch	P—Kt3
7.	KtxKtP	

The Knight cannot be captured, for Black would lose a Rook.

7.	. . .	Kt—Kt2

Counterattacking the Queen, thus preventing a discovered check. However, White announces mate in seven.

8.	B—B7 ch !

Sacrificing the Bishop in order to force the Black King onto a square where it will be exposed to a double check.

8.	. . . .	KxB
9.	Kt—K5 double ch	K—K3
10.	Q—B7 ch	K—Q3
11.	Kt—B4 ch	K—B4
12.	Q—Q5 ch	K—Kt5
13.	P—R3 ch	K—R5
14.	P—Kt3 mate.	

There are numerous examples of this stratagem.

GAME NO. 21

Three Knights' Opening

DR. MICHELSON   X.

(*Without the Queen's Rook*)

1.	P—K4	P—K4
2.	Kt—KB3	Kt—QB3

3.	Kt–B3	P–B4 ?
4.	P–Q4	BPxP
5.	KKtxP	Kt–B3
6.	KB–B4	P–Q4
7.	KtxQP	KtxKt
8.	Q–R5 ch	P–Kt3
9.	KtxP	Kt–B3

After Black's 9th move

10. B–B7 ch !   KxB ?

The game could not be saved even if Black had declined the sacrifice, e.g., 10. ... K–Q2; 11. Q–B5 ch, K–Q3; 12. B–KB4 ch, and wins. After the text move, White announces mate in three.

11.	Kt–K5	K–K2 (or K3)
	double ch	
12.	Q–B7 ch	K–Q3
13.	Kt–B4	
	mate.	

The same stratagem gave rise to a very amusing game in the second French Championship Tournament:

GAME NO. 22

Vienna Game

Played on September 4, 1924, at Strasbourg

FRED LAZARD   R. CREPEAUX

Fred Lazard (1883–1948), born in Paris, was the most all-round master in France. Not only was he an excellent tournament player, but also a renowned problem composer who won many prizes in competitions. His fame as an end-game composer is world-wide.

Robert Crepeaux was born at Grasse (France) in 1900 and has been Champion of France three times, in 1924, 1925 and 1941.

Crepeaux excels in combinative play, and the game he won against von Holzhausen (correspondence match, France–Germany, 1930) was published in Chess magazines throughout the world.

1.	P–K4	P–K4
2.	Kt–QB3	Kt–KB3
3.	P–B4	P–Q4
4.	BPxP	KtxP
5.	Kt–B3	Kt–QB3
6.	B–K2 ?	

The sequel will show that White should have played 6. B–Kt5.

6.	. . .	KB–B4 !
7.	P–Q4	KtxQP

Sacrificing a Piece to remove White's King's Knight.

8.	KtxKt	Q–R5 ch
9.	P–Kt3	KtxP
10.	Kt–B3	

Preventing a discovered check, but a second sacrifice will enable Black to give a double check.

10. ...   B—B7 ch
11. KxB

Otherwise, 11. K—Q2, Q—B5 ch, etc.

A Famous Game

11. ...   Kt—K5 double ch
12. K—K3   Q—R3 ch
13. resigns.

Or else Black mates, wins the Queen, or collects enough material to crush his opponent. For the sake of practice, the reader will do well to look for these variations on his own.

Innumerable Chess textbooks published since 1914 have quoted the following game as typifying the power of the double check. It was played in Vienna, 1910, between those two famous international masters R. Réti and X. Tartakower.

GAME NO. 23

Caro–Kann

R. RÉTI   X. TARTAKOWER

Richard Réti (1889–1928), a Hungarian Grand Master, gave his name to an opening. He won a number of tournaments: Kassa, Budapest, Gothembourg, Teplitz-Schönau. He wrote several books on Chess and composed studies which are little masterpieces. His most famous book is New Ideas in Chess, in which he developed the ideas of the hypermodern school, which he himself helped to found with the co-operation of his fellow countrymen Gyula Breyer and A. Nimzovitch. He was one of the most talented players of his generation.

Xavier Tartakower was born in Rostov-on-Don in 1887 of Austro-Polish parents. He took part in numerous tournaments with much

success. His best achievements are: London, 1927; Vienna, 1923; and Hastings, 1946. He has written innumerable Chess articles and many books, of which the most famous is The Hypermodern Game of Chess. His brilliant style adds to the joy of his comments.

1. P—K4   P—QB3

The idea underlying this move is to be able to play P—Q4 without blocking the Queen's Bishop.

2. P—Q4   P—Q4
3. Kt—QB3   PxP
4. KtxP   Kt—B3
5. Q—Q3   P—K4

With an undeveloped game Black should not attempt to open a file, as an open line is always to the advantage of the player with the better development.

6. PxP   Q—R5 ch

Forced, if Black wants to win back his Pawn; of course, this move contributes still further to White's development.

7. B—Q2   QxKP
8. O—O—O !

Laying a very subtle trap.

8. . . .   KtxKt ?

Falling right into it; 8. . . . QxKt would have cost the Queen (9. R—K1). After 8. . . . KtxKt, Black was hoping for 9. R—K1, which would have gradually won back the Piece.

After Black's 8th move

9. Q—Q8 ch !

To be able to double check the King.

9. . . .   KxQ
10. B—Kt5 double ch   K—B2

If 10. . . . K—K1; 11. R—Q8 mate.

11. B—Q8 mate.

After the double check, which can only be countered by moving the King, the Rook or the Bishop mate according to the flight square chosen by the King.

Tartakower, commenting on this game in his *Breviary of Chess*, says: "Better than any spoken word, this game illustrates the power of the double check."

This game, with its spectacular Queen sacrifice, is so well known that we should not have quoted it but for the practical lesson it contains.

When the game was over, Réti, who was a very modest man, did not pretend to have been struck by a flash of inspiration. He had had a reminiscence. In Chess, as in any other sphere, it is the experience of others, supplemented by the knowledge of past generations, which make progress and creative efforts possible.

The sacrifice of the Queen to bring about a double check

has occurred many times in the history of Chess. A few games will illustrate this statement.

GAME NO. 24

London, about 1846

W. SCHULTEN   B. HORWITZ

1.	P—K4	P—K4
2.	B—B4	Kt—KB3
3.	Kt—QB3	P—QKt4

This is not a very safe gambit.

4.	BxKtP	B—B4
5.	P—Q3	P—B3
6.	B—QB4	Q—Kt3
7.	Q—K2	P—Q4
8.	PxP	O—O
9.	Kt—K4 ?	

Instead of playing this Knight twice in nine moves, it would have been better to prepare castling.

9. . . .	KtxKt
10. PxKt	BxP ch

Since the Queen will have to recapture, White's King's Bishop will soon be *en prise*.

11. QxB	Q—Kt5 ch
12. B—Q2	QxB
13. Q—B3	P—KB4 !

So as to open a file on the unprotected King.

14. PxP

White's position is already difficult.

14. . . .   BxP

Black develops another Piece and threatens a discovered attack on the Queen.

15. Q—KKt3

The Queen is safe now, but there is a thunderbolt in store for the King. In fact, Black announces mate in three.

After White's 15th move

15. . . .	Q—B8 ch !
16. KxQ	B—Q6 double ch
17. K—K1	R—B8 mate.

GAME NO. 25

Greco–Philidor Gambit

Played in London, between 1864–1885

E. FALKBEER   SIMPSON

(*Without the Queen's Knight*)

1. P—K4	P—K4
2. P—KB4	PxP
3. Kt—KB3	P—KKt4
4. B—B4	B—Kt2
5. P—Q4	P—Q3
6. Q—Q3	P—QB3
7. P—KR4	P—KR3
8. B—Q2	Q—B3
9. PxP	PxP
10. RxR	BxR
11. P—K5	PxP
12. PxP	Q—Kt2
13. O—O—O	Kt—K2?

White mates in three.

14. Q—Q8 ch !	KxQ
15. B—R5 double ch	K—K1
16. R—Q8 mate.	

GAME NO. 26

Scotch Opening
Played in Paris, 1864

MACZUSKI   I. KOLISCH

Baron Ignace von Kolisch (1837–1889) was born in Presbourg. He was a Grand Master with, unfortunately, too brief a career. He started to play at the Café de la Régence in Paris. At the Bristol Congress, 1861, he took seventh place; at the Emperor tournament, Paris, 1867, first place. His business, mainly banking, prevented him from taking part in many Chess competitions.

Maczuski was a young Polish player thought highly of at the Régence.

1. P—K4	P—K4
2. Kt—KB3	Kt—QB3
3. P—Q4	PxP
4. KtxP	Q—R5

This aggressive move is not to be recommended, especially to beginners. Instead of this premature Queen move, it is better to develop a minor Piece, e.g., 4. . . . Kt—KB3.

5. Kt—B3	B—Kt5
6. Q—Q3	Kt—B3
7. KtxKt	QPxKt
8. B—Q2	BxKt
9. BxB	KtxP

Black got what he wanted, a Pawn, but his development is very backward.

10. Q—Q4 !	Q—K2
11. O—O—O	Q—Kt4 ch

This is a pointless check. Much better would have been . . . KtxB, followed by . . . castles. Kolisch must have underestimated his opponent.

12. P—B4 !	QxP ch
13. B—Q2	Q—Kt5

After Black's 13th move. Mate in 3

14. Q—Q8 ch !   KxQ
15. B—Kt5 double ch   K—K1
16. R—Q8 mate.

GAME NO. 27

Rosentreter Gambit

AWET   X.

1. P—K4	P—K4
2. P—KB4	PxP
3. Kt—KB3	P—KKt4
4. P—Q4	P—Kt5
5. Kt—K5	Q—R5 ch
6. P—Kt3	PxP
7. QxP	P—Kt7 dis ch
8. QxQ	PxR = Queen
9. B—K3	P—Q3
10. Kt—QB3	PxKt
11. O—O—O	Q—B6
12. B—Q2	B—QKt5
13. PxP	B—Kt5 ?
14. Q—Q8 ch !!	KxQ
15. B—Kt5 double ch	K plays
16. R—Q8 mate.	

These five games are of un-
equal merit. Réti's game is
elegant, short and precise, but
lacks in originality as the position is very similar to the one
obtained by Awet and its
mechanism can be retraced to
that of Horwitz and Falkbeer.
The latter, however, brought
about the position. Maczuski,
Awet and especially Réti
merely exploited a position
created by their opponents.

The previous game has by

no means closed the series, as
the following game will show:

GAME NO. 28

Caro-Kann Defense

*Played at Antwerp, 1931, in a
simultaneous blindfold display*

G. KOLTANOWSKI   N. N.

G. Koltanowski, originally a Pole,
lived in Belgium, of which country
he became Champion several times.
He never was a first-class master,
specializing largely in simultaneous
exhibitions, and above all in blindfold play. On May 30, 1931, at
Antwerp, he played thirty simultaneous blindfold games (twenty
won and ten drawn); and in Octo-
ber, 1937, he beat the world's record at Edinburgh with thirty-four
completed games in twelve hours
(twenty-four won and ten drawn
without a single loss). He is now
an American citizen and lives in
the United States. The world's record is now held by the Argentinian
Champion, Najdorf, who played
forty-five simultaneous blindfold
games in Brazil.

1. P—K4	P—QB3
2. P—Q4	P—Q4
3. Kt—QB3	PxP
4. KtxP	Kt—B3
5. B—Q3	

Sacrificing a Pawn to speed
up his development.

5. . . .	QxP
6. Kt—KB3	Q—Q1
7. Q—K2	B—B4
8. KtxKt ch	KtPxKt

9. BxB	Q—R4 ch
10. B—Q2	QxB
11. O—O—O	Q—K3

Threatening White's RP and also threatening to exchange Queens, with a Pawn up. This move looks strong, as it seems impossible to parry both threats simultaneously.

12. Q—Q3 !

White has now prepared his mating battery; and the only thing required is for Black to fall into the trap, which he does readily, proving that in a blindfold game the blinder of

White to play

The Evergreen

the two players is sometimes the one who sees!

12. . . .	QxP ?
13. Q—Q8 ch	KxQ
14. B—R5 double ch	K plays
15. R—Q8 mate.	

Here is another splendid example of the power of the double check:

END-GAME NO. 4

Café de la Régence, 1922

V. PLACE   N. N.

1. KtxP !	KxKt
2. P—Q5	B—Kt5

Black imagines that this pin is a sufficient defense.

3. RxKt ! !   BxQ

To be able to mate his opponent, White must bring his Rook to KR8. It seems impossible at first, but three consecutive double checks make it.

4. R—Kt6 double ch	K—R2
5. R—Kt7 double ch	K—R1
6. R—R7 double ch	K—Kt1
7. R—R8 mate.	

The present survey of the double checkmate would be incomplete if it did not include the famous "Evergreen." In the *Cinéma des Échecs* the French Master Alphonse Goetz wrote that every good amateur should know this game by heart.

In German Chess literature this game between Anderssen and Dufresne is known as the "Immergrün." It has figured in practically every anthology since Anderssen's death; and it is described poetically by Steinitz as "The Master's Laurel Crown"!

GAME NO. 29

Evans Gambit

Berlin, 1854

G. A. ANDERSSEN   J. DUFRESNE

G. Adolf Anderssen, of Breslau (1818–1879), professor of mathematics, was a German Grand Master and one of the best players of his epoch. He won first prizes in the London tournaments of 1851 and 1862, and in the Baden tournament of 1870; he beat Harrwitz, Kolisch, Löwenthal and Zukertort in matches. He was considered World Champion from 1851 until 1858, when Morphy beat him. His combinations were marked by genius.

Jean Dufresne, of Berlin (1828–1892), was a strong German player and author of various books and collections of master games. Thanks to these, many generations have learned the game of Chess.

1. P—K4   P—K4
2. Kt—KB3,   Kt—QB3
3. B—B4   B—B4
4. P—QKt4

The Evans gambit was introduced by the British naval captain W. D. Evans (1790–1872), and for a long time was considered "a gift of the Gods." The object of the Pawn sacrifice is to gain time and create a center, which is White's object in all variations of the Italian opening.

For many years the accepted gambit had given White a very strong attack. It has, however, disappeared from tournament play ever since Emanuel Lasker demonstrated that, by giving back the gambit Pawn, Black could obtain a superior end-game.

4. . . .   BxKtP
5. P—B3   B—R4

Nowadays, the following variation is very often played: 5. . . . B—B4; 6. castles, P—Q3; 7. P—Q4, B—Kt3!; 8. PxP, PxP; 9. QxQ, KtxQ; 10. KtxP, Kt—B3; with a small advantage for Black. At that time, however, not even a master would have dreamed of exchanging Queens at such an early stage of the game in order to obtain a better end-game, because the main object in view was a quick mating attack.

6. P—Q4   PxP
7. O—O   P—Q6

An innovation of Dufresne's.

8. Q—Kt3   Q—B3
9. P—K5   Q—Kt3

It is clear that the gain of a Pawn would cost Black a Piece, e.g., 9. . . . KtxP; 10. R—K1, P—Q3; 11. KtxKt, PxKt; 12. Q—R4 ch, winning the Bishop.

10. R—K1   KKt—K2
11. B—R3   P—Kt4

This sacrifice is intended to free the Queen's wing, as Black's position is rather cramped.

12. QxP

The best move! White now threatens: 13. BxKt, and therefore Black is unable to castle (if 13. . . . KtxB; 14. QxB).

12. . . .   R—QKt1
13. Q—R4

Maintaining the threat.

13. . . .   B—Kt3

Meeting the threat.

14. QKt—Q2   B—Kt2?

Black should castle without delay.

15. Kt—K4   Q—B4?

More waste of time.

16. BxQP

Threatening to win the Queen by Kt—B6 or Kt—Q6 ch, thus showing the absurdity of Black's last move.

16. . . .   Q—R4
17. Kt—B6 ch! PxKt
18. PxP

White has a magnificent attacking position, but as there is no immediate danger, Black takes the opportunity of counterattacking on the open KKt's file.

18. . . .   R—Kt1

This move threatens 19. . . . QxKt! with a mating attack.

After Black's 18th move

19. QR—Q1!

This quiet move is the prelude to a decisive attack. Dufresne may well be excused for having missed its significance.

19. . . .   QxKt

Black is two Pieces up and is also threatening mate. He is therefore entitled to think that, were White's attack to become too strong, he might equalize by giving back some of the material. Emanuel Lasker and Lipke took part in a debate to ascertain whether 19. . . . RxP ch did or did not refute this extraordinary combination. This controversy has raged since 1904— Chess is sometimes a difficult game!

After Black's 19th move

We shall now be able to understand 19. QR–Q1. By means of a Queen sacrifice White will drive the enemy King to a square where it will receive a fatal double check. The combination is complicated but sound. For this reason a whole century has not lessened the admiration of all Chess players.

20. RxKt ch   KtxR

If 20. . . . K–B1; 21. R–K3 dis ch wins the Queen. If 20. . . . K–Q1; 21. RxP ch, K–B1 (. . . KxR; 22. B–K2 dis ch wins the Queen); 22. R–Q8 ch and wins; because, if . . . RxR; 23. PxQ, or if . . . KxR; 23. B–K2 ch; and if . . . KtxR; 23. QxP, as in the game.

21. QxP ! ch   KxQ

And now the King is exposed to a double check.

22. B–B5 double ch   K–K1

If K–B3; 23. B–Q7 mate.

23. B–Q7 ch   K–Q1
24. BxKt mate.

CHAPTER 3: *The Smothered Mate*

A smothered mate is one in which the mated King is deprived of all its flight squares by its own Pieces or Pawns. It is delivered by a Knight.

Diagram of the smothered mate

Black is mated

The smothered mate can take place directly if the King is already blocked in by its own Pieces or indirectly when the attacker forces his opponent to block the flight squares of the King.

GAME NO. 30

English Opening

(HERE IS A MADE-UP EXAMPLE OF A SMOTHERED MATE)

1.	P—QB4	Kt—QB3
2.	P—K3	Kt—Kt5 ?
3.	Kt—K2 ? ?	Kt—Q6 mate.

It seems that White has asked to be mated

With the aid of a pin, a smothered mate can occur in one of the opening variations of the Caro-Kann defense.

GAME NO. 31

Caro–Kann Defense

Munich, 1932

ARNOLD   BOHM

| 1. | P—K4 | P—QB3 |

2. P—Q4   P—Q4
3. Kt—QB3   PxP
4. KtxP   Kt—Q2

With the idea of playing Kt—KB3, without allowing his Pawns to be doubled if there should follow an exchange.

5. Q—K2

Ingeniously preventing Black from carrying out his plan.

5. ...   KKt—B3??
6. Kt—Q6 mate.

Black is mated

The King's Pawn is pinned and cannot take the Knight. Alekhine managed to secure exactly the same mate against four opponents during a con-

sultation game, held in 1936 in the Balearic Islands.

Here is another example:

GAME NO. 32

Scandinavian Defense

Rotterdam—Leyde Match, 1933

G. OSKAM   W. DEMMENDAL

1. P—K4   P—Q4
2. Kt—KB3   PxP
3. Kt—Kt5   B—B4
4. Kt—QB3   Kt—KB3
5. Q—K2   P—B3
6. QKtxP   QKt—Q2?
7. Kt—Q6 mate.

There is also the threat of a smothered mate in a variation of the Budapest gambit. Here it is:

GAME NO. 33

Budapest Gambit

1. P—Q4   Kt—KB3
2. P—QB4   P—K4
3. PxP   Kt—Kt5
4. B—B4   B—Kt5 ch
5. Kt—Q2   Kt—QB3
6. Kt—B3   Q—K2
7. P—QR3   KKtxKP!
8. PxB??   Kt—Q6 mate.

The Smothered Mate of Damiano

It is also possible to obtain a smothered mate against a castled King. The device consists in forcing the King into a corner of the board and, by means of a sacrifice, compelling his own Pieces to obstruct his flight squares.

END-GAME NO. 5

P. DAMIANO, 1512

P. Damiano, a chemist from Odemira, Portugal, was famous for his Chess treatise, printed for the first time in Rome in 1512.

White mates in 2

1. QxP ch   QxQ
2. Kt—B7 mate.

It is a simple position. The idea of the sacrifice is twofold: to snatch away the Queen from the defense of Black's KB2, and to unpin the mating Knight.

It would be wrong to suppose that such an obvious combination cannot occur in prac-

tice. Here is a pleasant example:

END-GAME NO. 6

Manchester, 1929

ATKINSON   X.

White to play and win

1. RxB   QxR
2. Kt—Kt5   Q—Kt3
3. RxP ch   QxR
4. Kt—B7 mate.

The two first moves bring about Damiano's position, and the two last moves, Damiano's smothered mate. One cannot, however, announce mate in four because the Black Queen is not forced to capture the Rook on the first move.

The Mate of Lucena

We now come to a typical position in which a Queen sacrifice forces an obstruction to the opponent's King. The oldest example on record is Lucena's mate (1497). It is one of the first things one shows to beginners; and it never fails to produce the most profound admiration. In fact, it is this elementary combination which has initiated many amateurs into the artistry of the game of Chess.

END-GAME NO. 7

LUCENA, 1497

Juan Ramirez Lucena, a Spaniard, was famous for a work which he published in 1497 and for the *Manuscripts of Gottingue and Paris*, a revised version of the former.

White to play and mate in 5

1. Q—K6 ch   K—R1

Note how characteristic it is in all positions of this kind that the retreat of the King into the corner is practically forced. In fact, if . . . K—B1; 2. Q—B7 mate.

2. Kt—B7 ch   K—Kt1

The idea of these two consecutive checks is to force the King to a square where it will receive a double check—the idea being to obtain a double control of Black's KKt's square.

3. Kt—R6 double   K—R1
   check

Having obtained this double control, White sacrifices the Queen, forcing its capture by the Rook and thus causing the King's flight squares to be blocked.

4. Q—Kt8 ch !   RxQ
5. Kt—B7 mate.

Lucena's mate is constantly met in light games and in simultaneous displays. Masters place it as often as the Legal mate.

First of all, here is an old example given by Greco (1612) in his manuscript *Treatise of the Noble and Military Game of Chess, Containing Many Beautiful Moves and the True Science of the Game*, by Joachim le Calabrais.

GAME NO. 34

Giuoco Piano

(SIXTEENTH CENTURY VARIATION)

X.   **J. GRECO**

Joachim (Gioachino) Greco, called "the Calabrais," was born at Cellino, about 1600, and died in South America in 1634. He was the strongest European player of the seventeenth century, and published a treatise, which for one hundred and fifty years was the handbook of all Chess students.

1.	P—K4	P—K4
2.	Kt—KB3	Kt—QB3
3.	B—B4	B—B4
4.	O—O	Kt—B3
5.	R—K1	O—O
6.	P—B3	Q—K2
7.	P—Q4	PxP
8.	P—K5	

The maneuvers of both sides after the fifth move were not the best. Instead of the aggressive text move, 8. PxP would have been better, taking control of the center.

8. . . .	Kt—KKt5
9. PxP	KtxQP
10. KtxKt	Q—R5
11. Kt—KB3	

To avoid being mated, White should have played 11. B—B4.

11. . . .	QxBP ch
12. K—R1	Q—Kt8 ch
13. RxQ	Kt—B7 mate

We now come to a modern game played by two Swiss players: Q. Renold and R. Agassiz in 1903. An exact repeti-

After White's 11th move

tion of this game took place at the Régence in 1905 between Davril and Martin Saint-Léon. Later on, Constant Bernard found many an opportunity to play it.

The game also shows how this mate can be given with the King not necessarily in the corner of the board.

GAME NO. 35

Quade Gambit

Lausanne, 1903

Q. RENOLD   R. AGASSIZ

1.	P—K4	P—K4
2.	P—KB4	PxP
3.	Kt—KB3	P—KKt4
4.	Kt—B3	P—KKt5
5.	Kt—K5	

This is Quade's gambit. The usual move is 5. B—B4 (Muzio—MacDonnell gambit).

5. . . .	Q—R5 ch
6. P—Kt3	PxP
7. QxP	P—Kt7 ch ?

A mistake which beginners should be careful to avoid. It is sheer folly to attempt to win a Piece, even a Rook, with a backward development. We shall see how, in this particular position, Black's newly promoted Queen will be unable to defend his King. In Chess one should not only think in terms of Pieces, but also of position.

| 8. QxQ | PxR=Q |
| 9. Q—R5 | B—K2 |

Black really believes that he can keep the material he has won at the cost of only a Pawn and a check.

| 10. KtxBP | Kt—KB3 |

A useless counterattack. After the text move, White forces mate in three.

11. Kt—Q6	K—Q1
double ch	
12. Q—K8 ch	R or KtxQ
13. Kt—B7 mate.	

We could go on quoting dozens of examples of this kind of mate. Morphy, Bird and many other good players have used the same mating pattern often. But, as most of these games are similar, the reader can gain nothing new by studying them.

END-GAME NO. 8

DR. C. HARTLAUB, *about* 1904

Black to play and mate in 7 moves

This is a position from a brilliant game played by Dr. Hartlaub.

| 1. . . . | BxP ch |
| 2. RxB | |

Forced. If the King goes to R1, 2. . . . Kt—Kt6 ch; 3. PxKt, Q—R3 or 4 mate.

2. . . .	Q—B8 ch
3. R—B1	Q—K6 ch
4. K—R1	

If 4. R—B2, QxR ch; 5. K—R1, Q—B8 mate.

| 4. . . . | Kt—B7 ch |
| 5. K—Kt1 | |

Or 5. RxKt, Q—K8 ch; 6. R—B1, QxR mate.

5. . . .	Kt—R6 double ch
6. K—R1	Q—Kt8 ch
7. RxQ	Kt—B7 mate.

It is obvious that a good player will not let this happen to him, unless he is the victim of an oversight. But the threat of this mate can be the starting point of a winning position, as the following game will show.

GAME NO. 36

English Opening

Ostend International Tournament, 1907

O. S. BERNSTEIN   J. METGER

Ossip S. Bernstein was born in 1882 at Schitomir (Ukraine). He became a Grand Master and won the first prize at Ostend in 1906, but has played little tournament Chess since 1914. However, his second prize in London, 1946, shows that he has not forgotten it.

1. P—QB4	P—K4
2. Kt—QB3	Kt—KB3
3. P—KKt3	P—Q4
4. PxP	KtxP
5. Kt—B3	QKt—B3
6. B—Kt2	Kt—Kt3
7. O—O	B—K2
8. P—QR3	B—K3
9. P—Q3	O—O
10. P—QKt4	P—B3
11. B—Kt2	Q—B1

With the idea of exchanging Bishops (. . . B—R6). It would have been better, however, to have played 11. . . . Q—Q2.

| 12. R—B1 | R—Q1 |
| 13. Kt—K4 | Kt—B5 |

A complicated maneuver for exchanging minor Pieces.

| 14. Q—B2 | KtxB |
| 15. QxKt | |

White is now exerting a very strong pressure on the Queen's wing and is threatening, moreover, to advance the QKt Pawn.

15. . . .	B—R6 ?
16. BxB	QxB
17. P—Kt5	Kt—R4
18. Q—R2 ch	K—R1
19. RxP	R—Q2

Thus, Black hopes to free the game. There is, however, the threat of a smothered mate, although not apparent, and this enables Bernstein to win the game in a few moves.

    20. Kt(4)—Kt5 ! !

Threatening the Queen and also the mate of Lucena. (21. Kt—B7 ch . . . , 22. Kt—R6 double ch . . . , 23. Q—Kt8 ch . . . , 24. Kt—B7 mate.)

After Black's 19th move

20. . . .	PxKt
21. RxR	QxR
22. KtxKP	resigns.

Because of the following variations: 23. . . . Q–Q1; 24. Kt–B7 ch, wins the Queen. Or 23. . . . Q–K1; 24. Kt–B7 ch, followed by 25. Kt–Q6 dis ch, also wins the Queen.

The next diagram will show

END-GAME NO. 9

White to play and mate in 3

a particular aspect of the smothered mate which we have not yet met, but which, in our opinion, can occur in practice as a threat.

1. Kt–R6

Threatening 2. KtxP mate. There is only one answer.

1. . . .	R–KB1
2. R–Kt8 ch !	RxR
3. KtxP mate.	

We shall continue this chapter with a game which won first prize in a competition of imaginary games, organized by the Hampstead and Highgate Press.

GAME NO. 36A

Ruy Lopez

1. P–K4	P–K4
2. Kt–KB3	Kt–QB3
3. B–Kt5	Kt–B3
4. O–O	KtxP
5. P–Q4	B–K2
6. Q–K2	Kt–Q3
7. BxKt	KtPxB
8. PxP	Kt–Kt2
9. Kt–B3	O–O
10. R–K1	R–K1
11. R–Q1	Kt–B4
12. Kt–Q4	B–R3 ?
13. Q–Kt4	Q–B1
14. B–R6	B–B1
15. Kt–B5	Kt–K3
16. Kt–K4	K–R1
17. Kt–B6 !	PxKt
18. PxP	BxB

After Black's 18th move

We have now reached the end-game No. 9 position. White mates in four.

19. KtxB   R—B1

If 19. . . . Kt—Kt4; 20. QxKt and wins.

20. Q—Kt8 ch !   RxQ
21. KtxP mate.

CHAPTER 4: *"The Guéridon" Mate and the "Épaulettes" Mate*

Certain mates have been given picturesque names, such as, "Guéridon" and "Épaulettes." Guéridon in French means an occasional table, and it is thus called because, as will be seen in the next diagram, the Black and White Pieces form a rough sketch of a small table. They are typical positions, although they happen accidentally, not as a consequence of a weakening of the castled position or a central attack on the King.

A Typical Aspect of the Guéridon Mate

Black is mated

When the two corner squares behind the King are obstructed by its own Pieces and when the hostile Queen controls the six others adjacent to the King, the position is called the "Guéridon" mate on account of the resemblance of the position to a small table, as we have already mentioned. This mate, which may come as a result of many positions, may be forced at the very early stages of the game if one of the players makes a bad blunder. The following game is an amusing example:

GAME NO. 37

Philidor Defense

1.	P—K4	P—K4
2.	Kt—KB3	P—Q3
3.	B—B4	B—K2
4.	P—Q4	PxP
5.	KtxP	Kt—Q2 ?

44

After Black's 5th move

Black is mated

Black's last move is a serious mistake. Why? 1) Because it blocks the Queen and Queen's Bishop. 2) Because Black's K3, as a consequence, is weakened.

If White manages to force the advance of Black's KB Pawn or the capture of it, Kt–K6 would win the Queen. This idea forms the basis of the following maneuver.

6. BxP ch   KxB

Forced, if Black does not want to lose the Queen.

7. Kt–K6 !

White takes control of the weak square. If Black accepts the sacrifice, then mate in two.

7. . . .   KxKt
8. Q–Q5 ch   K–B3
9. Q–B5 mate.

This is the "Guéridon" mate. If Black had declined the sacrifice, he would have lost the Queen.

7. . . .   Q–K1
8. KtxBP   Q–Q1
9. Q–Q5 ch

White could also have played: 9. Q–R5 ch, P–Kt3; 10. Q–Q5 ch, K–B3; 11. B–Kt5 ch, K–Kt2; 12. Kt–K6, and wins.

9. . . .   K–B1

If . . . K–B3 or Kt3, 10. Q–B5 mate.

10. Kt–K6 ch   K–K1

Hoping, as a compensation, to win two minor Pieces for the Queen, but Black only succeeds in being mated. After the better 10. . . . K–B2; 11. KtxQ ch, and wins. (The best move, of course, is *10. . . . re-signs.*)

| 11. KtxP ch ! | K—B1 |
| 12. Kt—K6 ch | K—B2 |

Or *11. K—K1; 12. Q—R5* mate.

| 13. Q—R5 ch | King plays |
| 14. Q—B5 mate. | |

The Épaulettes Mate

When the mated King is obstructed to the right and to the left by its own Pieces, on a rank or on a file, we get the "Épaulettes" mate.

The next diagram will illustrate this better than any explanation.

(A)

(B)

(C)

Black is mated

(A) is a classical position. (B) shows a central position of the same mate. And (C) shows this mate being delivered by a Knight.

The following amusing game finishes with an "Épaulettes" mate delivered at a distance.

GAME NO. 39

Giuoco Piano

Played in 1904 at the Vienna Chess Club

A. ALBIN   O. S. BERNSTEIN

A. Albin (1848–1915) was born in Bucharest and lived in Vienna. He was a second-rate master. He gave his name to the Albin gambit.

1. P–K4	P–K4
2. Kt–KB3	Kt–QB3
3. B–B4	B–B4
4. Kt–B3	P–Q3
5. P–Q3	Kt–B3

In spite of what is generally believed, the "Giuoco Piano," a favorite with beginners, can sometimes lead to a very sharp fight, in which the slightest mistake may prove fatal.

6. B–KKt5

This move, popular in the Nineties and since then abandoned for B–K3, was reintroduced by Canal at Carlsbad in 1929 and also by Becker, Gild, etc. Capablanca used it himself in his game against Eliskases (Moscow, 1936).

6. . . .   B–K3

Nowadays one plays in preference 6. . . . Kt–QR4 or simply 6. . . . P–KR3. For instance: 7. BxKt, QxB; 8. Kt–Q5, Q–Kt3!; 9. QKtx P ch, K–Q; 10. KtxR, QxKtP; 11. KR–B1, B–Kt5; 12. Kt–R4?, BxP ch; 13. RxB, Q–Kt8 ch; 14. R–B1, Q–K6 ch ("épaulettes!"); 15. Q–K2, QxQ mate.

7. Kt–Q5	BxKt
8. BxB	P–KR3
9. BxKt ch	PxB
10. BxKt	

A modern player would not exchange his two Bishops so easily. At the time this game was played, Albin was fifty-six and Bernstein twenty-two.

10. . . .   QxB

Black has the advantage.

| 11. P–QB3 | R–QKt1 |
| 12. P–QKt4 | |

The Gunsberg–Albin–Mason style which makes even a beginner smile nowadays.

| 12. . . . | B–Kt3 |
| 13. Q–R4 | |

The player with an inferior development should never attack. Bernstein is about to remind his worthy opponent of this principle.

After White's 13th move

13. . . .   P—Q4!

Defending the attacked Pawn and counterattacking at the same time.

14. PxP   P—K5
15. PxKP   QxP ch

And now the King must start a very unpleasant pere-grination.

16. K—K2   Q—B5 ch
17. K—K1

17. K—Q1 would not have saved the game.

17. . . .   QxKP ch
18. K—B1   O—O
19. QxBP

White has an extra Pawn and a lost game.

19. . . .   KR—K1
20. K—Kt1   R—K3

An original way of bringing the Rook into play.

21. Q—Q7?

Foolishly aggressive. The text move is absolutely incom-patible with White's position and leads him to his ruin. A little better would have been 21. Q—R4, although the game is quite hopeless.

21. . . .   R—Q3
22. Q—R4   Q—K7
23. R—KB1

After White's 23rd move

23. . . .   QxKt
24. PxQ   R—Kt3 mate.

White's last move is not forced; it is the acceptance of the sacrifice which allows the "Épaulettes" mate.

END-GAME NO. 10

C. M. DE LABOURDONNAIS, 1833

White to play and mate in four

This device, however artificial it may seem, is sometimes put into practice. Here is an end-game by Blackburne which uses it to force a "Guéridon" mate.

END-GAME NO. 11

Played at Kiddermaster in 1863 during a simultaneous blindfold exhibition

BLACKBURNE   **X.**

This is position No. 22 in Labourdonnais' *Treatise*; it has been specially composed to show how a series of checks forces the obstruction of the Black King's neighboring squares.

White mates in 3

1. Kt—K6 ch   K—K1
2. Q—Q8 ch   BxQ

The first "Épaulette."

3. R—B8 ch   RxR

The second "Épaulette."

4. Kt—Kt7 mate.

1. P—Kt4 ch !   BxP
2. B—Kt6 ch !   PxB
3. QxR mate.

This is the lateral aspect of the "Guéridon" mate.

CHAPTER 5: *Greco's Sacrifice*

A complete description of Greco's mate would need at least a hundred pages and cannot, therefore, be included in this book, especially as this sacrifice does not necessarily lead to a forced mate.

GAME NO. 40

French Defense

(FROM A CHESS BOOK PUBLISHED IN 1619)

G. GRECO   X.

1.	P—K4	P—K3
2.	P—Q4	Kt—KB3
3.	B—Q3	Kt—B3
4.	Kt—KB3	B—K2
5.	P—KR4	O—O
6.	P—K5	Kt—Q4

After Black's 6th move

It is hardly necessary to emphasize the fact that Black has played very badly, but it was the ingenious Greco, or one of his contemporaries (one was not very particular about small details like that in the seventeenth century!), who had the merit of discovering the combination (BxP ch) which, in this position, gives an immediate and winning advantage to White.

This attack has been systematically studied for the last forty years. The first essay to be published on this subject was written by the Swiss master Ervin Voellmy (Vom Rochade-Angriff, *Révue Suisse d'Échecs*, 1911). In it the author describes the necessary conditions which have to exist for the sacrifice to take place. Unfortunately, most people who have studied this sacrifice have omitted to mention this important essay.

Greco's analysis of the position is very superficial, and we shall therefore try to supplement it in every possible detail.

7. BxP ch   KxB

Black may refuse the sacrifice, in which case White can withdraw his Bishop and be content with the extra Pawn, or he may play 8. Kt—Kt5 and give increased momentum to the attack; this was suggested by Greco himself and we also think that this continuation is far stronger.

8. Kt—Kt5 ch

After White's 8th move

Black has now three lines of play:

1) The withdrawal of the King to Kt1.
2) The capture of the Knight.
3) The further advance of the King to his Kt3 or R3.

We shall analyze all three continuations.

Withdrawal of the King

8. . . .   K—Kt1

Obviously not 8. . . . K—R1; 9. Q—R5 ch, and mate next move.

9. Q—R5   BxKt

If 9. . . . R—K1; 10. Q—R7 ch, K—B1; 11. Q—R8 mate. Or: 9. . . . Kt—B3; 10. PxKt, R—K1; 11. Q—R7 ch and 12. Q—R8 mate.

10. PxB   P—B4

The only move (except 10. P—B3) which meets the double mating threat (11. Q—R7 or R8 mate), because it gives a flight square to the King.

11. P—Kt6   Q—R5
12. QxQ   plays
13. Q—R8 or R7 mate.

Capture of the Knight

8. . . .   BxKt
9. PxKt dis ch   K—Kt3

If 9. . . . K—Kt1; 10. Q—R5, P—B4; 11. P—Kt6. (See the above-mentioned variation.)

    10. Q—R5 ch   K—B4
    11. Q—R3 ch   K—Kt3

If 11. . . . K—K5; 12. Q—Q3 mate.

    12. Q—R7 mate.

Further advance of the King

    8. . . .   K—Kt3

If 8. . . . K—R3; 9. KtxP double ch wins the Queen.

    9. P—R5 ch   K—R3

If 9. . . . K—B4; 10. P—Kt4 mate.

    10. KtxP double ch   K—R2
    11. KtxQ

White has won the Queen for two minor Pieces and should win the game blindfold.

The Greco position is brought about by an artificial series of moves which seems abnormal to the modern player, and we thought the game had been specially composed by Greco until the day one of the authors of this book had the opportunity to play the following light game:

GAME NO. 41

Alekhine Defense

Played at the Nice Chess Club, June 16, 1923

G. RENAUD   X.

1. P—K4	Kt—KB3
2. P—K5	Kt—Q4
3. P—Q4	P—K3 ?
4. Kt—KB3	B—K2
5. B—Q3	O—O ?
6. P—KR4	P—QB4
7. BxP ch	K—R1

The day before, the very same opponent had played 7. KxB and had been mated.

8. Kt—Kt5	P—Kt3
9. P—R5 !	K—Kt2

If 9. . . . BxKt; 10. PxP, K—Kt2; 11. Q—R5 !, BxB; 12. B—Kt8, RxB; 13. Q—R7 ch, and mate follows.

After Black's 12th move

10. Q—Kt4   P—B4
11. KtxP ch   PxKt
12. QxP ch   K—R1

With a Piece up and the King in the corner, Black thinks that the game is saved.

13. B—Kt8 !

A typical sacrifice. White threatens mate and if 13. . . . RxB, 14. Q—R6 mate.

13. . . .   R—B2
14. BxR   resigns.

As the mate can be delayed but not avoided.

We should not have published this mediocre game but for the opportunity it gave us to analyze the continuation following 8. Kt—Kt5.

General Aspect of the Greco Mate

Diagram A

White to play

This is the barest possible aspect of the Greco position, where there is the minimum number of Pieces required for the attack and for the defense. This position is even more simplified than Greco's, for there is no Rook's Pawn for White, making it impossible to open the KR column to reinforce the attack. Moreover, Black's Q2 and K2 are not obstructed.

Let us see what happens when the sacrifice is accepted, supposing the Black King to withdraw to Kt1.

1. BxP ch   KxB
2. Kt—Kt5 ch   K—Kt1
3. Q—R5   R—K1

The only defense.

White mates in 5

In this position White announces a forced mate because:

1) Black's K1 and Q1 are obstructed.

2) Black's Q3 and KB3 are controlled by a White Pawn and offer no refuge to the King.

4. QxP ch

In order to leave the White Queen in full control of the seventh rank where the mate will take place.

4. . . .	K–R1
5. Q–R5 ch	K–Kt1
6. Q–R7 ch	K–B1
7. Q–R8 ch	K–K2
8. QxP mate.	

The Greco Mate

Black is mated

If Black has an extra Piece for the defense, it will also be necessary for White to have an extra Piece for the attack.

Diagram B

White to play

In this second diagram, White has a R's Pawn supported by a Rook and Black the K's Bishop.

1. BxP ch	KxB
2. Kt–Kt5 ch	K–Kt1
3. Q–R5	

It would be useless to play 3. . . . R–K1 because Black's K2 is obstructed. Therefore Black must play:

| 3. . . . | BxKt |

When the conditions described in either diagram A or B are fulfilled, the withdrawal of the King to Kt1 or R1 enables White to mate or to win the Queen for two minor Pieces.

It is beyond the scope of this book to analyze the consequences of the advance of the King to Kt3. Let us only insist on the fact that this sacrifice is correct and must lead sooner or later either to a mate, to some material advantage or to an attack which largely compensates for the loss of the sacrificed Bishop. In any case, the general line of play following the King's advance to Kt3 must consist in bringing the Queen to Kt4 or Kt3 with the threat of a discovered check by removing the Knight to a square where it can attack the Black Queen at the same time. And also to bring the Queen's Knight to the King's wing via B3 and K2.

CHAPTER 6: Quizzes

It is not sufficient to possess an extensive knowledge of mating devices. One must also be able to put that knowledge into practice, and to recognize in every position the mating possibilities, wherever they are to be found, even if they are not immediately obvious. For this reason we have decided to give the reader some practical quizzes, solutions for which he will find at the end of the book.

We shall give some practical tips for the solving of these quizzes; but this will depend, of course, on the strength of the reader. If he is a strong player, he should not place the Pieces on the board, but should examine the diagram, analyze the position mentally and find the solution. If, on the contrary, he is a weaker player, it may be necessary for him to place the Pieces on the board. But even then he should attempt to

solve the problem without moving the Pieces, bearing in mind that he is playing against an imaginary opponent.

Do not forget that Chess is played with the mind and not with the hands!

On the other hand, once the solution has been found mentally, it is necessary to check it carefully by moving the Pieces. Experience has taught us that it facilitates the task of memorizing the variations if one actually shifts the Pieces himself. That holds good for many players.

These quizzes do not necessarily correspond chronologically to the chapters studied.

All the positions are not artificially composed; some are taken from real games, which makes them more interesting and instructive. These mates have actually been delivered, or might have been, if the player had been aware of the possibility.

56

We have done our best to indicate the date and place of the game from which the position was taken. It has not al- ways been possible, for many authors have been very negligent on this point.

EXERCISE NO. 1
St. Petersburg, 1909

FORGACS   TARTAKOWER

White mates in 2

EXERCISE NO. 2

X.   D. JANOWSKI

Black mates in 2

EXERCISE NO. 3
About 1904

G. MAROCZY   X.

White mates in 2

EXERCISE NO. 4
Toward 1860

CH. MAURIAN   X.

White mates in 2

EXERCISE NO. 5

1834

BOURDONNAIS   MAC DONNELL

White mates in 2

EXERCISE NO. 6

Y.   X.

White mates in 2

EXERCISE NO. 7

Y.   X.

White mates in 2

EXERCISE NO. 8

Consultation Game, Riga, 1898

LURIE and E.   J. B. and
WAGEHEIM   O. B.

White mates in 3

EXERCISE NO. 9

Blindfold Game, Before 1904

V. MARIN   X.

White mates in 2

EXERCISE NO. 10

STEINBRECHER   X.

White mates in 3

EXERCISE NO. 11

Philadelphia, 1862

X.   G. H. DERRICKSON

Black mates in 3

EXERCISE NO. 12

X.   MAC CUTCHEON

Black mates in 3

EXERCISE NO. 13

EXERCISE NO. 14
Hastings, 1933

X.   P. KENDE   TYLOR   WINTER

Black mates in 4   White mates in 4

EXERCISE NO. 15
(*Composed Position*)
PH. STAMMA, 1737

EXERCISE NO. 16
(*Composed Position*)
ERCOLE DEL RIO

White mates in 6   White mates in 7

Part II

TYPICAL MATES

In this part we shall study the principal mating positions against a castled King. The classification of these mates is based more on convenience than on theory.

Wherever possible, we have given the mate a name; and where one exists (e.g., "Anastasia," "Arabian"), we have kept it; where no name exists, we have named the mate after the first famous player who used it.

We shall be very grateful to readers who can supply us with further particulars on the authors of these mates.

CHAPTER 1: The Corridor Mate

(NO. 1)

This is the simplest of all mate diagrams.

Mate No. 1

White mates in 2

The Black King is hemmed in on the last rank by three of its own Pawns and can only move sideways. The King's square is weak because it is only protected by the Rook and doubly threatened by the White Queen and Rook. The mating maneuver is both simple and spectacular.

1. Q—K8 ch   RxQ
2. RxR mate.

The final position of the "corridor mate" is characteristic.

Black is mated

It is obviously the weakness of the last rank that enables such a mate to take place. If Black, for instance, had another Piece on this rank, Queen or Rook, this mating maneuver would be impossible.

It may frequently happen that the King itself protects the mating square.

63

Mate No. 1A

White to play and mate in 3

In this case, the mate is only delayed.

1. Q—K7 ch   K—Kt1
2. Q—K8 ch   RxQ
3. RxR mate.

In the following diagram, there is a trap to be avoided. If Black is aware of it, White cannot mate, and given the

symmetry of the position and the equality of the material, Black must draw.

White must not try to be brilliant by sacrificing the Queen. After 1. Q—Kt8 ch, Black does not reply 1.... RxQ which loses, but plays 1....Q—B1 with a drawn result.

There is a simple win by the natural move—

1. R—Kt8 ch   RxR

There is no hope in 1. ... Q—B1; 2. RxQch, and White has a Queen for a Rook.

2. QxR ch   Q—B1
3. R—B8

White wins the Queen.

END-GAME NO. 12

White to play

GAME NO. 42

Sicilian Defense
London Tournament, 1851

A. ANDERSSEN   M. WYVILL

Marmaduke Wyvill was a strong English master who took second place, behind Anderssen, in the first international tournament (London, 1851).

1. P—K4   P—QB4
2. B—B4

A modern player would never dream of the text move in this opening, as Black can close the Bishop's diagonal (. . . P—K3).

2. . . .   Kt—QB3
3. Kt—QB3   P—K3
4. P—Q3   Kt—K4

It is better to develop other Pieces.

5. B—B4

This, on the contrary, is a very modern move; Steinitz's followers would have withdrawn the King's Bishop to Kt3 in order to avoid doubled Pawns. Anderssen prefers to carry on with his development.

5. . . .   KtxB

This maneuver is a pure waste of time, for this Knight has already moved three times.

6. PxKt   P—QR3

A precaution, as 7. Kt—Kt5 would be disastrous. White has already a strategically won game; his development is vastly superior and he controls the Queen's file and center squares.

7. Q—K2   Kt—K2
8. O—O—O   Kt—Kt3
9. B—Kt3   B—K2

10. P—B4   O—O
11. P—B5   B—Kt4 ch

A roundabout way for regrouping his Pieces.

12. K—Kt1   PxP
13. PxP   R—K1
14. Q—Kt4   Kt—B1

The Knight has found a refuge.

15. Kt—B3   B—B3
16. Kt—K4   P—QKt4

Seeking a counterattack on the Queen's wing.

After Black's 16th move

One need not be much of an expert to see that White has much the better game:

1) His three minor Pieces and his Queen are in action.

2) His Rooks are in communication and ready to intervene.

3) He has an evident gain in space.

On the contrary, Black, with the exception of his King's Bishop, has his Pieces playing a strictly defensive part.

But to transform this positional advantage into something concrete requires a lot of ingenuity, and it is at this juncture that combinational play has a predominant part.

17. **B—B7 !**

Black cannot accept this sacrifice. If 17. . . . QxB, 18. KtxB ch, K—R1; 19. KtxR, threatening simultaneously mate (20. QxP mate) and the Queen (20. KtxQ), it is clear that both threats cannot be parried at the same time.

Although it involves the loss of the exchange, the best defense is 17. . . . RxKt; 18. QxR, QxB; 19. QxR.

17. . . .   Q—K2

Black has not foreseen the dramatic consequences of this retreat.

18. KtxB ch   QxKt
19. R—Q6 !

The Queen has no retreat. If 19. . . . Q—K2; 20. P—B6!, threatening mate and winning the Queen. To avoid

After White's 19th move

this, Black will have to give up a Piece.

19. . . .   Kt—K3
20. PxKt   QPxP
21. KR—Q1

White develops his last inactive Piece.

21. . . .   B—Kt2
22. R—Q7   B—B3
23. B—K5

After White's 23rd move

Without hesitation, Black should have attempted to exchange Queens; notwithstanding the strength of his opponent and the danger of his position, he tries a countercombination in order to regain his Piece.

23. . . .   BxKt
24. Q—Kt3

"A very fine move," assures a contemporary commentator. We think, however, that 24. QxB would have been quite as strong, and after 24. . . . QxB, would have allowed the same combination as in the game, in a more accurate and effective manner.

24. . . .   Q—Kt3
25. QxB   PxP
26. QxR   RxQ

26. . . . P—B3 could not have saved the game.

27. R—Q8 ch   RxR

28. RxR mate.

This is a distinct example of the corridor mate No. 1. Let us point out that in the illustrative games we give, the mating maneuver may be somewhat different from the ones we give in the beginning of the chapter. In this game, for instance, the Queen captures a Rook without giving check, but the principle remains the same, as the object is to weaken Black's first rank by destroying one of the defenses. All the necessary mating conditions shown in diagram No. 1 exist in the Anderssen–Wyvill game.

The next diagram will show that in spite of a double defense of Black's first rank, a

Mate No. 1B

After Black's 25th move

White to play and mate in 3

Queen sacrifice makes it possible to mate.

1. QxR ch   RxQ
2. R—K8 ch   RxR
3. RxR mate.

It is not always necessary for the King to be hemmed in by three Pawns, as will be shown in the next diagram:

Mate No. 1C

White to play and mate in 2

In certain cases, this threat may compel the opponent to resign, as in the following endgame:

If White's Bishop were on his QB8, then 1. B—K6 ch, Q—B2; 2. QxQ ch, K—R1; 3. QxB ch, RxQ; 4. RxR mate. But White's Bishop is not where it should be. This, how-ever, did not prevent Réti from forcing the win.

END-GAME NO. 13

New York, 1924

R. RÉTI   E. D. BOGOLJUBOFF

After Black's 24th move

24. B—B7 ch   K—R1

If 24. . . . QxB; 25. QxQ and mate in two.

25. B—K8 !   resigns.

Because mate can only be avoided at the cost of a Piece, in a position which offers no compensation for the loss.

As we shall see in many other examples, the threat of a typical mate can win the game, even if it is possible to parry that threat, but at too high a price.

CHAPTER 2: *Variation of the Corridor Mate*

(NO. 2)

The corridor mate is, as we have seen in the previous chapter, based on the weakness of the opponent's first rank. With this second aspect of the corridor mate, we have another element: the weakness of a given square.

Mate No. 2

White to play and mate in 3

This position is often met in practice. Black's Bishop's Pawn is only defended twice, by King and Rook, and three

times attacked, by the Queen and both Rooks.

Furthermore, Black's first rank is weak, as it is only defended by one Rook; these conditions enable White to sacrifice his Queen and to force mate in two moves.

1. QxP ch   RxQ
2. R—B8 ch   R—B1
3. RxR (any R) mate.

The weakly defended BP and the weakness of Black's first rank have allowed this mate to take place, and the final position is the one of the corridor mate.

In this case the pin allows mate in two.

1. QxP ch   RxQ
2. R—Q8 mate.

The procedure is exactly the same. The only difference is the pinned Rook, which helps to speed up the mate.

Mate No. 2A

White to play and mate in 2

The student may think that nothing short of a serious blunder could enable one to reach such a mate in practice. This is only partially true. Such a position may be forced in consequence of a whole series of weak moves.

Here are three examples:

GAME NO. 43

Queen's Pawn Opening

International Team Tournament, Hamburg, 1930

SIR G. THOMAS   F. J.
MARSHALL

Sir G. Thomas was several times British Champion.

F. J. Marshall (1877-1944) was a brilliant attacking player and for many years U. S. Champion. He was first at Cambridge Springs, 1904, and at Scheveningen, 1905.

1. P–Q4	Kt–KB3
2. P–QB4	P–K3
3. Kt–KB3	P–QKt3
4. P–K3	B–Kt2
5. B–Q3	Kt–B3

A move which denotes an insufficient grasp of the position.

6. Kt–B3	B–Kt5
7. B–Q2	O–O
8. O–O	P–Q4
9. R–B1	Q–K2
10. PxP	PxP
11. Q–B2	QR–Q1
12. P–QR3	BxKt
13. BxB	Kt–K5
14. P–QKt4	P–QR3

White was threatening to play P–Kt5, winning the exchange or the QBP.

15. B–Kt2	R–Q3

In spite of his inferior position, Marshall wants to attack at all costs.

16. Kt–K5	R–R3
17. P–B3	KtxKt
18. QPxKt	Q–R5 ?
19. P–Kt3	Q–Kt4

Or 19. . . . . KtxP; 20. PxKt, Q–R8 ch; 21. K–B2, Q–R7 ch; 22. K–K1, and White is a Piece up.

20. PxKt	QxP ch
21. Q–B2 !	QxB
22. RxP	B–B3

After Black's 22nd move
White announces mate in 4

23. QxP ch   RxQ
24. R—B8 ch   B—K1
25. RxB ch   R—B1
26. RxR mate.

GAME NO. 44

Giuoco Piano

(MOELLER ATTACK)

Cheltenham, 1913

C. V. LOYE   F. U. BEAMISH

In Chess congresses, particularly in England, it is customary for subsidiary contests to take place. The following game was played between two second-rate players who, nevertheless, seem to be pretty well versed in the opening theory, as the first sixteen moves will show.

1. P—K4   P—K4
2. Kt—KB3   Kt—QB3
3. B—B4   B—B4
4. P—B3   Kt—B3
5. P—Q4   PxP
6. PxP   B—Kt5 ch
7. Kt—B3   KtxP

8. O—O   BxKt
9. P—Q5

This is the Moeller attack, which is extremely powerful, and has been the object of constant analysis. Although it is impossible to ascertain its precise value, in exchange for the sacrificed Pawn White obtains a position with considerable winning chances.

9. . . .   B—B3
10. R—K1   Kt—K2
11. RxKt   O—O
12. P—Q6 !   PxP
13. QxP   Kt—B4
14. Q—Q5   P—Q3

Black can draw by repeating the same moves, as after 14 . . . Kt—K2, White has no better alternative than Q—Q6.

15. Kt—Kt5 !   BxKt
16. BxB

Up to now both players have followed a well-known variation, but at this juncture, Black, less up to date than White, falls headlong into the trap.

16. . . .   QxB ? ? ?

The usual move is 16. . . . Q—B2. We have now reached the typical mate No. 2 position.

After Black's 16th move

17. QxP ch   RxQ
18. R—K8 mate.

This game is all the more instructive because it shows how futile it is to memorize a long opening variation, when, as soon as one is left to one's own resources, one blunders and is unable to foresee a mate in two moves.

Here is an example of the world champion forced to resign on account of the threat of mate No. 2.

GAME NO. 45

Ruy Lopez

Margate Tournament, 1937

P. KÉRÉS   A. ALEKHINE

A. Alekhine was born in Moscow in 1892, became a French citizen in 1929, and died at Lisbon in 1946. He was a Chess master at the

age of fifteen, and a Grand Master at the age of twenty. He became World Champion after defeating Capablanca at Buenos Aires in 1927. He is considered the greatest Chess genius of the twentieth century, and his games are regarded as priceless gems. But it is impossible to describe his style in a few lines.

Paul Kérés was born at Narva (Estonia) in 1916. He showed a marked aptitude for the game as a youth and in 1937 he was publicly acknowledged a Grand Master. In 1938 he shared first prize with R. Fine at the "Avro" Tournament, the strongest ever held. In 1940, he beat Euwe in a match.

1. P—K4	P—K4
2. Kt—KB3	Kt—QB3
3. B—Kt5	P—QR3
4. B—R4	P—Q3

This defense was played by Lange-Schultz in 1863 and is now called "the Steinitz defense deferred," as it was especially recommended by Steinitz. It has been very successful for a long time.

5. P—B4 !

But this move, tried for the first time by Duras against Vidmar and Janowski (Carlsbad, 1907) in a similar position (5. P—Q3, Kt—B3; 6. P—B4) seems somewhat to invalidate the Steinitz defense deferred, as most of the recent games have been won by White.

The text move has a double object. It prevents Black from driving away the Bishop on R4 by . . . P—QKt4, and it gives White control of his Q5.

| 5. . . . | B—Q2 |
| 6. Kt—B3 | P—KKt3 |

Several other continuations have been suggested, but unsuccessfully so far.

7. P—Q4 !

This move must be played at once, before Black takes control of his Q5.

| 7. . . . | B—Kt2 |

In the radio match game Boleslawski–Fine, Black played 7. . . . PxP, but after 8. KtxP, B—Kt2; 9. KtxKt, PxKt; 10. castles, Kt—K2; 11. P—B5 !, with a decisive advantage for White.

| 8. B—K3 | Kt—B3 |
| 9. PxP | PxP |

Black recaptures with the Pawn in order not to simplify the position by an early exchange of Pieces. Capablanca always sought simplification. Alekhine retained this fighting spirit all his life.

10. B—B5 !

Preventing Black from castling on the King's side.

| 10. . . . | Kt—KR4 |

The idea is to bring this Knight to Q5 via B5 and K3.

| 11. Kt—Q5 | Kt—B5 |
| 12. KtxKt | PxKt |

Black's King's Bishop springs into life again.

13. P—K5

Sacrificing a Pawn to obstruct the diagonal once more.

| 13. . . . | P—KKt4 |

It might have been possible for Black to accept the sacrifice, but not without danger. For instance: 13. . . . KtxP; 14. KtxKt, BxKt; 15. Q—K2. The text move, however, weakens Black's position, which is already very tricky.

| 14. Q—Q5 ! | B—KB1 |

If 14. . . . P—Kt5; 15. P—K6, BxKP (not 15. . . . PxP; 16. Q—R5 mate); 16. BxKt ch, with a winning attack.

| 15. BxB | RxB |

Without this Bishop, Black's position becomes weak.

16. O–O–O   Q–K2

To be able to castle Queen without any loss of time.

17. BxKt !

Black is not given the slightest break.

17. . . .   BxB
18. Q–Q3   B–Q2

Giving up a Pawn in order to castle.

19. KtxP !   O–O–O

Obviously not 19. QxKt; 20. QxB mate.

20. Kt–B3   P–KB3
21. PxP   RxP
22. KR–K1   Q–Kt5 ? ? ?

A colossal blunder. Not even world champions are proof against such mistakes!

After Black's 22nd move

23. QxB ch !   resigns.

Or else:

23. . . .   RxQ
24. R–K8 ch   R–Q8
25. RxR mate.

Resulting in corridor mate No. 2.

CHAPTER 3: *Greco's Mate*

(NO. 3)

Mate No. 3

White to play and mate in 2

In the diagram, Black's castled position is very much weakened for the following reasons:

1) The King's Knight is not there.

2) The White Bishop's diagonal is opened on the King's position, on account of Black's Pawn on B3. In fact, if Black did not have the KR Pawn, White could mate in one move. This suggests the following maneuver whereby

White forces the opening of the mating file:

1. Kt—Kt6 ch   PxKt
2. R—R1 mate.

The following diagram shows the final position of this mate.

Pattern of mate No. 3

Black is mated
The King might also be placed on Black's R2.

This mating device is to be found in a variation by Gioachimo Greco, in a book of his published in 1619. Here it is!

GAME NO. 46

Giuoco Piano

G. GRECO

1.	P—K4	P—K4
2.	Kt—KB3	Kt—QB3
3.	B—B4	B—B4
4.	P—B3	Kt—B3
5.	Kt—Kt5	O—O
6.	P—Q3	P—KR3 ?
7.	P—KR4	PxKt ?
8.	PxP	Kt—R2
9.	Q—R5	R—K1
10.	QxBP ch	K—R1

After Black's 10th move

11. RxKt ch

In this game the opening of the file is even more brutal than in our previous example. Not only is Black compelled to capture the Rook, but he must do so with his King.

11.	. . .	KxR
12.	Q—R5 mate.	

A few modern games will serve as further illustrations.

GAME NO. 47

Queen's Gambit Declined

Chicago, 1899

JOHNSON   F. J. MARSHALL

Marshall's opponent was a strong American amateur.

1.	P—Q4	P—Q4
2.	P—QB4	P—K3
3.	Kt—QB3	Kt—QB3

A strange move in this position, obstructing the QBP.

4.	Kt—B3	Kt—B3
5.	B—B4	B—Q3
6.	B—Kt3	Kt—K5

Marshall's intention is to build up a stonewall defense, but it is a very doubtful idea, as White's Queen's Bishop is in action and Black's QBP is obstructed.

7.	P—K3	O—O
8.	B—Q3	P—B4
9.	P—QR3	P—QKt3
10.	R—B1	B—Kt2

Black does not seem to have calculated the consequences of the following exchange:

11.	PxP	PxP
12.	KtxP !	

Black must not dream of winning the Knight on account of 12. . . . BxB; 13. RPxB, QxKt?; 14. B—B4, winning the Queen. Black therefore tries another maneuver, which, however, turns out to be incorrect.

12. . . .   KtxQP
13. B—QB4

A very strong move because it not only threatens a double check but attacks the Queen's Knight twice over. Marshall hopes to find a way out.

13. . . .   KtxKt ch
14. PxKt   KtxB

After Black's 14th move

White is now in a position to place Greco's Mate No. 3.

15. Kt—K7 double ch   K—R1
16. Kt—Kt6 ch   PxKt
17. PxKt ch   Q—R5
18. RxQ mate.

GAME NO. 48

Dutch Defense

Baden-Baden, 1925

E. GRÜNFELD   C. TORRE

Ernst Grünfeld, of Alekhine's generation, is an excellent Austrian master, universally known for his knowledge of openings. He has won prizes in nearly all the tournaments held before the last war.

Carlos Torre, born in 1906, is a Mexican player, first heard of in this tournament. For several years he played brilliantly and seemed to have a great future; but illness has since kept him from Chess.

1. P—Q4   P—K3
2. Kt—KB3   P—KB4
3. P—KKt3

This line of play has been specially recommended by Grünfeld and has become very popular.

After Black's 11th move

3. . . .	Kt–KB3
4. B–Kt2	P–Q4

Torre intends to build up a stonewall.

5. O–O	B–Q3
6. P–B4	P–B3
7. Q–B2	O–O
8. P–Kt3	Kt–K5
9. B–Kt2	Kt–Q2
10. Kt–K5	Q–B3
11. P–B3	KtxKt
12. PxQKt??	

An amazing mistake for such an experienced master as Grünfeld. It was necessary to play 12. PxKKt, Kt–Kt5, with a complicated position for both sides.

12. . . .	B–B4 ch
13. K–R1	

And now Black can apply mate No. 3.

13. . . .	KtxP ch
14. PxKt	Q–R3 ch
15. B–R3	QxB mate.

GAME NO. 49

Sicilian Defense

Played in the nineteenth century

J. COCHRANE   X.

J. Cochrane, an English player of the early nineteenth century, published a book (1822) and introduced the gambit which bears his name.

1. P–K4	P–QB4
2. P–Q4	

This premature advance of the Queen's Pawn was tried by Cochrane against H. Staunton in 1844. Nowadays one plays 2. Kt–KB3.

2. . . .	PxP
3. QxP	Kt–QB3
4. Q–Q1	

White has lost a tempo. 4. Q–K3 seems better.

4. . . .	P–K4

This is certainly a faulty move. Black's backward Queen's Pawn becomes weak and his Q3 a hole.

5. B–QB4	Kt–B3
6. Kt–KB3	Q–R4 ch

Useless, White is now able to regain the lost tempo.

7. B–Q2	Q–Kt3
8. B–B3	B–B4
9. O–O	O–O
10. KtxP	KtxP
11. Q–B3	KtxB

A serious mistake. Necessary was 11. . . . KtxKt.
White now mates in four.

12. BxP ch	RxB

If 12. . . . K–R1; 13. Kt–Kt6 ch, PxKt; 14. Q–R3 mate (mate No. 3).

After Black's 11th move

13. QxR ch   K—R1
14. Q—K8 ch   B—B1
15. QxB mate.

Black has avoided mate No. 3 . . . but he gets mated in the corridor manner instead!

A typical mate can recur throughout a whole game as a basic idea. The next game will serve to illustrate this point.

GAME NO. 50

Ruy Lopez
Breslau, 1859

A. ANDERSSEN   MAX LANGE

Max Lange (1832–1889), a strong German player, was the author of many textbooks from which innumerable players have learned the principles of Chess. He also left a collection of Morphy's games, which was considered the best extant until Maroczy's appeared. Two variations of the Giuoco Piano bear his name.

1.	P—K4	P—K4
2.	Kt—KB3	Kt—QB3
3.	B—Kt5	Kt—Q5
4.	KtxKt	PxKt
5.	B—B4	Kt—B3
6.	P—K5	P—Q4 !
7.	B—Kt3	B—KKt5
8.	P—B3	Kt—K5 !
9.	O—O	

If White takes the Bishop, he exposes himself to a very violent attack. For instance: 9. PxB?, Q—R5 ch; 10. P—Kt3 (if 10. K—K2, Black mates in two),KtxKtP, etc., and the position of the White King is disastrous.

9. ....   P—Q6 !

In order to get an open diagonal for his King's Bishop.

10. PxB ?

A very bad mistake; 10. Q—K1 undoubtedly would have been better. After the text move, Black is going to try for the Greco mate, and this threat weighs heavily on White for the next seven moves.

10. ....   B—B4 ch
11. K—R1

If the Black Queen were on its third rank, White could be mated in two moves (11. .... Kt—Kt6 ch, followed by 12.

Q—R3 mate). As it is, Black does not have the time to prepare this mate (if 11. . . . Q—Q3?, 12. Q—B3, covering his Kt3). Therefore, in order to prevent Q—B3, Black sacrifices his Knight. For eleven moves White fights desperately to delay the fatal issue.

After White's 10th move

11. . . .	Kt—Kt6 ch ! !
12. PxKt	Q—Kt4
13. R—B5 !	P—KR4
14. PxP	

Of course not *14*. RxQ, PxP dis ch; *15*. R—R5, RxR mate.

14. . . .	QxR
15. P—Kt4	Q—B7
16. P—Kt3	QxKtP
17. Q—B1	QxP

A modern player would resign, as the mate cannot be avoided, but one century ago the fight was carried on to the bitter end.

18. QxP ch	KxQ
19. BxP ch	K—K2
20. B—Kt2	Q—R5 ch
21. B—R3	QxB mate.

CHAPTER 4: *Greco's Mate*

(NO. 4)

Here is a mate, ending in the same way as Greco's mate No. 3; the mating attack, however, is somewhat different.

Mate No. 4

White to play and mate in 3

The conditions of this diagram are exactly the same as the ones in the diagram of mate No. 3, the only difference being that, instead of sacrificing a Piece to open the Rook's file, White forces the same result by means of a threat.

1. Q—R5   P—R3

Forced.

2. Q—Kt6!   PxKt

Also forced. Black captures the Knight and does away with the threat, but in so doing opens the mating file.

3. Q—R5 mate.

This is quite a classic maneuver and is frequently met in practice.

Pattern of mate No. 4

Black is mated

Here is a light game on this subject:

GAME NO. 51

Four Knights' Opening

Nice, 1941

X.   V. KAHN

1.	P—K4	P—K4
2.	Kt—KB3	Kt—QB3
3.	Kt—B3	Kt—B3
4.	P—Q4	PxP
5.	KtxP	B—Kt5
6.	KtxKt	KtPxKt
7.	B—Q3	O—O
8.	O—O	P—Q4

A logical move which neutralizes White's center.

9. P—K5?

This is a weak move. More usual is 9. PxP, PxP; 10. B—KKt5, P—B3, with equality.

9. . . .		Kt—Kt5
10. P—B4??		

A nasty positional mistake. The continuation should have been: 10. B—KB4, P—B3!, with advantage to Black. The refutation of the text move is not long in coming.

10. . . .		Q—R5
11.	P—KR3	B—B4 ch
12.	K—R1	Q—Kt6
13.	PxKt	Q—R5 mate.

Between strong players, this maneuver is out of the ques-

tion; but it can be used as a threat, or as a variation in a combination, as the next endgame will reveal.

END-GAME NO. 14

ROTLEVI   RUBINSTEIN

After Black's 21st move

Black has just played 21. . . . Q—R5, threatening mate. In the actual game, White played 22. P—KKt3, and that enabled Rubinstein to place a magnificent combination, starting with . . . RxKt. Black ought to have foreseen a much less aggressive defense: 22. P—KR3. In which case the game would have proceeded in this way:

22.	P—KR3	RxKt !
23.	BxR	BxB
24.	QxB	Q—Kt6
25.	PxKt	Q—R5 mate.

CHAPTER 5: *Anastasia's Mate*

(NO. 5)

Let us consider the following diagram. We notice that the only weaknesses in Black's castled position are the absence of the King's Knight and his undefended K2. This, nevertheless, is sufficient for White to launch a decisive attack, although the mating maneuver is not quite so apparent as in the previous diagrams.

White to play and mate in 3

1. Kt—K7 ch   K—R1
2. QxP ch ! !   KxQ
3. R—R1 mate.

With the first move, White forces Black to move his King and takes control of the two important squares; with the second, he opens the mating file and forces the Black King to his R2; with the third, he delivers mate.

This mate is called Anastasia's mate after a novel by Wilhelm Heinse, *Anastasia und das Schachspiel, Briefe aus Italien,* published in 1803. The next two diagrams show two aspects of the final position.

Diagram A   Diagram B
(*Mate No. 5*)   (*Mate No. 5*)

Black is mated

In diagram A mate is delivered against a castled King; in

diagram B, against a King in the center. However spectacular they may seem, these mates do not differ essentially from mates 3 and 4.

The following game was composed by E. Lasker and published in his book *Common Sense in Chess*, 1895. It will serve to show a practical example of Anastasia's mate.

GAME NO. 52

THEORETICAL VARIATION, COMPOSED IN 1894

Ruy Lopez

EMANUEL LASKER

Emanuel Lasker (1868–1940), Doctor of Philosophy, was World Champion from 1894 to 1921. His clear and precise style made him well-nigh invincible. He is perhaps the greatest Chess personality of the last fifty years.

1.	P—K4	P—K4
2.	Kt—KB3	Kt—QB3
3.	B—Kt5	Kt—B3
4.	O—O	KtxP
5.	R—K1	

This is not the best move, as it allows Black to equalize too quickly. 5. P—Q4 is much stronger. If, however, Black wants equality, he must beware of all the traps which this line of play involves.

5.	. . .	Kt—Q3
6.	Kt—B3	KtxB
7.	KtxP !	

Laying Black a very subtle trap.

7. . . .	KtxKKt ?

Another way of falling into the trap would be to take the Queen's Knight, e.g., 7. . . . KtxQKt; 8. KtxKt ch, B—K2; 9. KtxB, KtxQ; 10. Kt—Kt6 ch, Q—K2; 11. KtxQ, and White is a Piece up. The only right move is 7. . . . B—K2 !, furthering development and making discovered checks impossible.

8. RxKt ch	B—K2

White is going to exploit the pin of the Bishop and make it the basis of a mating combination.

After Black's 8th move

9. Kt—Q5 !

White prefers the double attack on the pinned Bishop to the recapture of the Piece.

9. . . .   O—O

Giving back the Piece to have his King in safety—or so he thinks.

10. KtxB ch   K—R1

If White were to play 11. RxKt, Black would answer 11. . . . QxKt, with equality. But there is no question of this.

11. Q—R5 !

This move is both simple and powerful. In fact, it wins the game. If Black, ignoring the threat, were to play, for instance, 11. . . . P—Q3, then 12. QxP ch, KxQ; 13. R—R5 mate (Anastasia's mate).

11. . . .   P—KKt3
12. Q—R6

This move threatens mate in two, and Black can only parry the threat at the cost of heavy material loss.

12. . . .   P—Q3
13. R—R5 !

Introducing another typical mate, which we shall study later on.

13. . . .   PxR
14. Q—B6 mate.

The following game shows the important part that time plays in a serious game. In tournament play time is limited, and usually each player is allowed fifteen moves to the hour. Time is checked first after two hours of play, and then hourly. A good player should therefore regulate his time so as to have some in reserve for complicated positions. It often happens that players are short of time when difficulties arise, and the middle-game often finds them with just a few seconds left to play the remaining moves.

GAME NO. 53

Queen's Pawn Opening

Carlsbad, 1929

M. VIDMAR   M. EUWE

M. Vidmar, born in 1885, is a Yugoslav professor and engineer. He is a Grand Master.

M. Euwe, born in Holland in 1901, was a professor of mathematics and is an international Grand Master. He is a very talented player who combines tactical gifts with profound theoretical knowledge. He defeated Alekhine in a match for the world title, which he kept for two years.

1. P—Q4   Kt—KB3
2. Kt—KB3   P—KKt3
3. B—Kt5

Vidmar often plays the openings carelessly and does not bother about theoretical considerations. The text move, for instance, is not to be recommended.

3. . . .   B—Kt2
4. QKt—Q2   P—B4
5. P—K3   P—QKt3
6. B—Q3   B—Kt2
7. O—O   P—KR3
8. B—KB4   P—Q3
9. P—B3

It was much better to play 9. P—KR3, to keep the Queen's Bishop.

9. . . .   Kt—R4
10. Q—Kt3

Clearly showing that he hopes to win in the middle-game, and that it is a matter of indifference whether his Pawn position is weakened.

10. . . .   KtxB
11. PxKt   O—O !
12. QR—Q1

Obviously not BxP on account of . . . P—B5, followed by . . . P—Q4.

12. . . .   Kt—B3
13. B—Kt1

If BxP, then . . . Kt—R4.

13. . . .   PxP
14. PxP   P—K3

If 14. . . . KtxP; 15. KtxKt, BxKt; 16. BxP, BxKtP; and Black has an extra Pawn but a very unpleasant position.

15. Kt—K4   Kt—K2
16. Q—R3   Kt—B4
17. R—Q2

Not 17. P—KKt4, Kt—R5; 18. KtxKt, QxKt; 19. KtxP ?, QxKtP ch, etc.

17. . . .   Q—K2
18. Kt—Kt3   KtxKt
19. BPxKt !

A rare case in which it is preferable to take with the BP, contrary to Philidor's principle.

19. . . .   KR—B1
20. P—KKt4   R—B2
21. P—B5   KPxP
22. PxP   P—KKt4
23. R—K1   Q—B3
24. P—R3   QR—QB1
25. R(2)—Q1

Defending the first rank.

25. . . .   R—B5

Both players are getting short of time, and time is going to be checked very soon. Under these circumstances not only is there danger of tactical mistakes, but the whole position may be misjudged. In this case, for instance, 25. . . . BxKt would have been sufficient for a draw.

26. P—Q5	P—QR4
27. Kt—Q2	Q—Q5 ch
28. K—R1	QxQP
29. B—K4	RxB
30. KtxR	QxBP

Both players have made it; but during the rush of the last five moves they thought White could not play 31. KtxQP on account of 31. QxP ch, quite forgetting that the Pawn is already defended by the White Queen. White has now a material advantage.

| 31. KtxQP | BxP ch |

Trying for a perpetual check.

| 32. KxB | R—B7 ch |
| 33. K—R1 | Q—B5 |

This seems to be a winning move, but White has already prepared a lovely mating combination.

| 34. R—K8 ch ! | B—B1 |

Forced, if Black does not want to lose a Rook.

| 35. RxB ch | KxR |

Or else Black loses the Queen.

| 36. Kt—B5 dis ch | K—Kt1 |
| 37. Q—B8 ch ! ! | resigns. |

After Black's 33rd move

After 37. . . . KxQ; 38. R—Q8 mate (Anastasia's mate).

GAME NO. 53A.

Dutch Defense

Played before 1900

X.   B. RICHTER

1. P—Q4	P—KB4
2. P—QB4	P—K3
3. Kt—KB3	Kt—KB3
4. P—K3	P—QKt3
5. B—Q3	B—Kt2
6. O—O	B—Q3
7. Kt—B3	Kt—B3
8. P—K4	PxP
9. KtxP	B—K2
10. Kt—K5	

A Pawn sacrifice, in order to attack Black's uncastled King, whose position is all the weaker because his KBP is missing.

10. . . .	KtxP
11. KtxKt ch	BxKt
12. Q—R5 ch	P—Kt3
13. BxP ch	PxB
14. QxP ch	K—K2
15. Kt—Kt4	Q—B1 !

Laying a trap. White, hoping to win the Queen or a Piece, falls blindly into it.

| 16. KtxB | QxKt |
| 17. B—Kt5 | |

And now Black announces mate in five.

| 17. . . . | Kt—K7 ch |
| 18. K—R1 | RxP ch |

After White's 17th move

19. KxR	R—R1 ch
20. Q—R6	RxQ ch
21. BxR	QxB mate.

CHAPTER 6: *Boden's Mate*

(NO. 6)

This mate usually occurs when one of the players has castled on the Queen's side.

White to play and mate in 2

Black's castled position is weakened by the advance of the Bishop's Pawn, and this gives White's Bishop full control of the diagonal. If Black's Knight's Pawn were not there, White could mate in one move by B—QR6. The mating maneuver will therefore consist in forcing the opening of the mating diagonal.

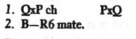

1. QxP ch	PxQ
2. B—R6 mate.	

Pattern of mate No. 6

Black is mated

This diagram shows that only two Bishops deliver mate, and that the mating maneuver consists in opening a diagonal instead of a file.

Here is a practical application of this mate:

GAME NO. 54

Center-Counter Game

This game was played in 1913 by two British amateurs

B. G. BROWN   A. G. ESSERY

1.	P—K4	P—Q4
2.	PxP	Kt—KB3
3.	P—Q4	QxP
4.	Kt—QB3	Q—QR4
5.	Kt—B3	B—Kt5
6.	P—KR3	BxKt
7.	QxB	P—B3
8.	B—Q3	QKt—Q2
9.	O—O	O—O—O

There was no need to castle on the Queen's side, especially in view of the fact that the QBP has moved. It is true that White's castled position is also weakened by the advance of the KRP, but this weakness is not immediately exploitable, as Black has exchanged his Queen's Bishop, whereas:

10. B—KB4

White takes immediate control of the weakened diagonal pointed toward the King's position.

10.	. . . .	P—K3
11.	P—R3	

Initiating a Pawn attack. When the Kings have castled on opposite sides, the player with the better development has usually a decisive advantage.

11.	. . . .	Q—Kt3

A very bad mistake. The better 11. . . . . Kt—Q4, however, was a losing move, too.

12.	Kt—R4	QxQP
13.	QxP ch	PxQ
14.	B—R6 mate.	

The following example is much more interesting.

GAME NO. 55

Four Knights' Defense

Scheveningen   Tournament, 1913

EDWARD LASKER   F. ENGLUND

Edward Lasker, born in 1885 in Germany, emigrated to the United States in 1914 and became an electrical engineer. He is a very well-known player, and made a reputation for himself with his book *Modern Chess Strategy* (1914), in which, for the first time, an author deals systematically with the conduct of the game.

F. Englund was a strong Swedish player.

1.	P—K4	P—K4
2.	Kt—KB3	Kt—QB3
3.	Kt—B3	Kt—B3
4.	B—Kt5	Kt—Q5

At the time this game was played, this old move, which has since been reintroduced by Rubinstein, had not been much analyzed and its true value not assessed.

5. KtxP

This continuation gives rise to terrific complications.

5. . . . Q—K2
6. Kt—B3

Nowadays one would prefer to play 6. P—B4, with a sharp struggle for both players.

6. . . . KtxP

This does not seem the best move. The correct continuation is 6. . . . KtxB; 7. KtxKt, QxP, with equality.

7. O—O—O ! KtxKt
8. QPxKt KtxKt ch
9. QxKt

White's better development is a compensation for his doubled Pawns.

After Black's 13th move

9. . . . Q—B4
10. R—K1 ch B—K2
11. B—Q3 P—Q4

12. B—K3 Q—Q3
13. B—KB4 Q—KB3

Black must have thought his troubles were over, and he is making ready to castle peacefully, but . . .

14. QxP ! P—B3

If Black castles, he loses the QBP, and if he accepts the sacrifice he loses the game, e.g., 14. . . . QxB; 15. B—Kt5 ch, P—B3 (if 15. . . . K—B1; 16. Q—Q8 ch, BxQ; 17. R—K8 mate); 16. BxP ch, PxB; 17. QxP ch, K—B1; 18. QxR, Q—B2; 19. R—K3, followed by QR—K1, with a winning position.

15. Q—K4

Preventing Black from castling King.

15. . . . B—K3
16. R—K3 B—QB4
17. B—K5 Q—R3
18. R—Kt3 B—KB1

If 18. . . . Q—Q7; 19. R—KB1, threatening 20. B—KB4 and Black has no defense.

19. R—Q1

It would have been better to have played 19. P—QB4 to prevent . . . B—Q4. Lasker was probably relying on his opponent's blundering, which is perhaps inadvisable but not forbidden by the rules.

19. . . .   O—O—O???

Lasker was right. Englund absent-mindedly castles on the Queen's side, forgetting about the opportunity he is giving White to play Boden's mate.

20. QxP ch   PxQ
21. B—R6 mate.

Here is a position taken from the Nimzovitch–Alekhine game played at the Vilna tournament of 1912 when Alekhine was nineteen years old.

A. NIMZOVITCH   A. ALEKHINE

After White's 15th move

White has just played 15. O—O—O, and in so doing has set a very subtle trap; in fact, if Black attempts to win a Pawn, this is what happens:

15. . . .   PxP
16. PxP   KtxP
17. RxKt   QxR
18. QxP ch   Kt—Q2

If 18. . . . R—Q2; 19. Bx R ch, KtxB; 20. Q—K8 mate.

19. Q—B6 ch   PxQ
20. B—R6 mate.

And this is the typical position of the Boden mate. Alekhine, of course, saw through the threat and played 15. . . . B—Q3 in time. But as can be seen, the latent threat of this mate prevented Black from capturing the Pawn.

Black to play and mate in 2

What is characteristic about the Boden mate is not so much the mate itself, but the maneuver which leads up to it.

The King need not necessarily have castled on the Queen's side for this mate to take place, as the next examples will show:

END-GAME NO. 15

About 1865

HARRWITZ   **F. HEALEY**

| 1. . . . | QxKt ch |
| 2. PxQ | B—R6 mate. |

END-GAME NO. 16

Simultaneous Exhibition, 1925

A. ALEKHINE   **X.**

White to play and mate in 2

| 1. QxP ch ! | PxQ |

If 1. . . . Q—K2; 2. QxQ mate.

2. B—Kt6 mate.

In this case the King is on its initial square.

And this is the final aspect of the Boden mate:

Mate No. 6A

White to play and mate in 2

| 1. QxP ch | PxQ |

If 1. . . . R—B2; QxR mate.

2. R—Kt8 mate.

In this last example it is a Rook which mates, and the final mating position differs quite considerably. But the principle remains the same.

CHAPTER 7: *Blackburne's Mate*

(NO. 7)

A castled King may be mated by a Bishop on R7, supported by a Knight on Kt5, provided the long black diagonal is controlled by a Bishop as in the next diagram:

Final aspect of mate No. 7A

Black is mated

Pattern of mate No. 7B

Black is mated

The Black King may also be in a corner.

Of course, there can be many other ways of disposing the Pieces, for instance:

Pattern of mate No. 7C

Black is mated

To obtain such a position, the attacker must not hesitate to sacrifice Pieces, even the Queen if necessary. For instance:

1. Q—R1   P—R4
2. QxP!   PxQ
3. B—R7 mate.

Mate No. 7A

White to play and mate in 3

The object of the Queen's sacrifice is, as in the Boden mate, to force the opening of the mating diagonal.

This mate, with or without the Queen sacrifice, is not rare. Let us start with the oldest one known:

GAME NO. 56

Jerome's Gambit

London, 1880

X.   J. H. BLACKBURNE

James Harry Blackburne (1842–1926) was one of Britain's strongest players from 1870 to 1914. For a long time he was champion of England. He excelled in simultaneous and blindfold Chess.

1. P–K4	P–K4
2. Kt–KB3	Kt–QB3
3. B–B4	B–B4
4. BxP ch	KxB

5. KtxP ch	KtxKt
6. Q–R5 ch	P–Kt3

The correct continuation is 6. . . . K–K3, but Blackburne relied on his opponent's inexperience.

7. QxKt	P–Q3 !
8. QxR	Q–R5
9. O–O	Kt–B3
10. P–QB3 ?	

After 10. Q–Q8 !, B–Kt3; 11. P–K5, PxP; 12. Q–Q3, White had the advantage.

10. . . .	Kt–Kt5
11. P–KR3	BxP ch
12. K–R1	B–KB4 !
13. QxR	

After White's 13th move

13. . . .	QxP ch
14. PxQ	BxP mate.

This is mate No. 7B.

And here are two examples of mate No. 7A:

GAME NO. 57

Bird's Opening

Played about 1880

H. E. BIRD   X.

H. E. Bird (1830–1908) was, from 1850 to 1900, one of the most brilliant English players. He had genius, but his lack of knowledge of positional play never enabled him to reach the first rank.

1.	P—KB4	P—Q4
2.	P—K3	P—QB4
3.	Kt—KB3	P—K3
4.	P—QKt2	Kt—QB3
5.	B—Kt2	Kt—B3
6.	P—QR3	B—K2
7.	B—Q3	O—O
8.	O—O	P—QKt3
9.	Q—K1	B—Kt2
10.	Q—R4	P—Kt3 ?

This game, except for a few inaccurate moves, has a very modern appearance; the last move, however, is definitely bad because it sadly weakens the King's position. Much better would be 10. . . . Kt—K5 !

    11. Kt—Kt5

threatening 12. BxKt, followed by 13. QxP mate.

    11. . . .   P—KR4
    12. P—KKt4 !   KtxP ?

The position now reached makes it possible to apply the Blackburne mating maneuver.

After Black's 12th move

Note that Black is still in possession of all his Pieces, including his Pawns, and that White is only minus the Pawn he has sacrificed.

    13. QxP   PxQ
    14. B—R7 mate.

Many amateurs have been the victims of this type of mate in simultaneous displays. The next game will show how a Grand Master, Salo Flohr, was caught in the same way.

GAME NO. 58

Queen's Pawn Opening

Bilin Tournament, 1930

S. FLOHR   R. PITSCHAK

Salo Flohr was born in Prague in 1909, and first started tournament Chess in 1929. He stood out immediately as one of the most formidable masters of his generation. A naturalized Russian during the second World War, he is at present one of the Grand Masters of the U.S.S.R.

Rudolf Pitschak, of Brünn, is a very strong Czech player.

1. P—Q4	Kt—KB3
2. Kt—KB3	P—K3
3. QKt—Q2	P—B4
4. P—K3	P—QKt3
5. B—Q3	B—Kt2
6. O—O	B—K2
7. P—B4	O—O
8. P—QKt3	P—Q4

By an inversion of moves the two players have almost reached the typical position of the Tarrasch defense of the Queen's gambit declined. The right continuation for White now is 9. B—Kt2, with equality.

| 9. Q—B2 | Kt—B3 |

Intending to play Kt—QKt5, thus exchanging the Knight for the attacking Bishop.

| 10. P—QR3 | BPxP |

Black takes advantage of the position of the White Queen to open the file and, later on, the diagonal by PxP.

11. BPxP	QxP
12. PxP	KtxP
13. Q—Kt1	

Demonstrating effectively how an inaccurate move (9.

Q—B2) gives Black the initiative.

| 13. . . . . | KR—Q1 |

Threatening to win a Piece by 14. . . . . KtxKt, followed by 15. . . . . QxB.

| 14. Kt—K1 | Q—KR4 |
| 15. B—Kt2 | |

Endeavoring to complete his development. But it is already too late. In view of Black's tactical threats, the right move is 15. Kt—B4.

| 15. . . . . | B—Q3 ! |
| 16. P—Kt3 | |

Or 16. P—R3, Q—K4; 17. P—Kt3, Q—Q4, etc.

| 16. . . . . | Kt—Kt5 |
| 17. P—KR4 | QxP ! |

After White's 17th move

And the typical Blackburne mate must follow if White

takes the Queen. If not, mate follows in any case, and so . . .

18. resigns.

Here is a game which reminds one of Blackburne's.

GAME NO. 59

Ruy Lopez
Munich, 1932

X.   S. TARRASCH

S. Tarrasch (1862–1934), of Breslau, was the strongest German master of Lasker's generation. A remarkable theorist, his teachings, clear and logical, although a little dogmatic, have contributed much to the game.

1. P–K4	P–K4
2. Kt–KB3	Kt–QB3
3. B–Kt5	P–QR3
4. B–R4	Kt–B3
5. O–O	B–B4
6. KtxP	KtxP
7. KtxKt	KtPxKt
8. Q–B3	Q–R5
9. Kt–B3	KtxKt
10. BxP	PxB
11. QxP ch	B–Q2
12. QxR ch	K–K2
13. QxR	

Since the "Immortal Game" was played, it is now known how dangerous it is, in certain positions, to capture the two Rooks with the Queen, since the latter gets out of play and

is no longer available for defense.

13. . . .	Kt–K7 ch
14. K–R1	BxP
15. P–KR3	

The only move. If 15. P–KKt3, B–B3 mate, and if 15. RxB, QxR, and mates next move. After the text move, Black mates in three.

15. . . .	QxP ch
16. PxQ	B–B3 ch
17. K–R2	B–Kt6 mate.

GAME FRAGMENT NO. 2

This mate often occurs as a threat in master play, as will be seen in the next example.
Berlin Tournament, 1926

E. COLLE   E. GRÜNFELD

After Black's 15th move

In the diagram position, Colle played 16. Kt–Kt5!,

and after 16. . . . P—Kt3?, sacrificed his Knight on his B7 and obtained a winning attack; this game, in fact, got a brilliancy prize. But after 16. Kt—Kt5, Colle must have also taken into consideration this delightful variation:

16.	Kt—Kt5	BxP
17.	P—Q5	PxP
18.	Kt—B5	B—B1
19.	Q—R5 !	KtxQ
20.	Kt—R6 ch	PxKt
21.	BxP mate.	

Resulting in Blackburne's mate.

To conclude this chapter let us quote a game which seems to have been composed, since the typical mating position is brought about in a very curious manner—the Knight coming to the attack of the besieged King after the sacrifice of the Queen.

GAME NO. 60

Giuoco Piano

(PUBLISHED WITHOUT INDICATION OF SOURCE)

(*Bulletin Ouvrier des Échecs*, MARCH, 1937)

1.	P—K4	P—K4
2.	Kt—KB3	Kt—QB3

3.	B—B4	B—B4
4.	P—B3	Kt—B3
5.	P—Q4	B—Kt3

5. . . . PxP was necessary.

6.	PxP	KKtxP
7.	Q—Q5	

White has a very clear advantage.

7.	. . .	BxP ch
8.	K—B1	O—O
9.	QxKKt	B—Kt3
10.	B—Q3	P—Kt3
11.	B—KKt5	Q—K1
12.	B—B6	P—Q4

The position we have reached is almost identical to the ones we have already studied, with the difference that the White Knight is not on his Kt5. However, this strange position of the Black Queen makes a Queen sacrifice possible.

13.	Q—R4	P—KR4
14.	QxP !!	PxQ
15.	Kt—Kt5	resigns.

The mate cannot be parried. If the Black Queen had been elsewhere, 15. . . . R—K1 would have given a flight square to the Black King.

CHAPTER 8: *Quizzes*

EXERCISE NO. 17

LABONNE   X.

White to play and mate in 2

EXERCISE NO. 18

Carlsbad Tournament, 1929

E. COLLE   JOHNER

Black to play and mate in 4

EXERCISE NO. 19

(Composed Position, pre-1802)

X.   X.

White to play and mate in 2

EXERCISE NO. 20

X.   DADIAN DE MINGRELIE

Black to play and mate in 3

EXERCISE NO. 21

Toward 1853

SCHULTEN   S. BODEN

Black to play and mate in 2

EXERCISE NO. 22

Toward 1875

PAREDES   VASQUEZ

Black to play and mate in 2

EXERCISE NO. 23

Toward 1880

MACKENZIE   X.

White to play and mate in 4

EXERCISE NO. 24

Paris, January, 1920

M. ROBINSON   E. CHATARD

Black to play and win

EXERCISE NO. 25

(*Composed Position*)

C. DE LA BOURDONNAIS, 1883

White to play and mate in 4

EXERCISE NO. 26

Before 1901

H. VON GOTTSCHALL   X.

White to play and mate in 5
or wins the Queen

EXERCISE NO. 27

Breslau, 1910

After F. J. MARSHALL

White to play and mate in 7

EXERCISE NO. 28

Paris Tournament, 1867 (Altered Position)

C. GOLMAYO   S. LOYD

Black to play and mate in 8

CHAPTER 9: *Mate No. 8*

The following diagram shows the irresistible strength of a simple KB Pawn reaching White's B6 and able to keep the square. This Pawn, which has sometimes more value than a Piece, controls the square Kt7, and if White plays the Queen to his R6, the threat (Q—Kt7, mate) is decisive. In the following position, for instance, Black's Pawn chain is intact, but White forces the fatal . . . P—Kt3.

Mate No. 8

White to play and mate in 3

1. P—B6   P—Kt3

The only move.

2. Q—R6   *ad lib.*
3. Q—Kt7 mate.

Lolli's Mates

Sometimes Black has time to move the King to R1, leaving the Knight square to the Rook and defending his Kt2. But if White has the necessary material, this defense is not sufficient, as the next example will show.

White threatened Q—R6, followed by Q—Kt7 mate.

1. . . .   K—R1
2. Q—R6   R—Kt1

In this position, however, the Rook deprives the King of a flight square.

3. QxP ch !   KxQ
4. R—R1 mate.

This Queen sacrifice dates

103

Mate No. 8A

Black to play
White mates in 3

from the eighteenth century
and is credited to Lolli. This
mate can also occur under a
slightly different form, making
use of a pin.

Mate No. 8B

White to play and mate in 3

   1. Q—R6   R—Kt1
   2. QxP ch !   KxQ
   3. R—R5 mate.

The pinned Pawn cannot

capture the Rook. This pin
can also occur laterally:

Mate No. 8C

White to play and mate in 3

   1. Q—R6   R—KKt1
   2. R—R8 !

Pinning the Rook.

   2. . . .   *ad lib.*
   3. Q—Kt7 mate.

To conclude this chapter,
we shall give two final aspects
of mate No. 8.

Pattern of mate No. 8

Black is mated

Pattern of mate No. 8A

Black is mated

CHAPTER 10: *Mate No. 9*

The next diagram shows the power of a White Bishop placed on White's KB6 or even, in certain cases, anywhere on the long diagonal. In fact, if the KR file were open, White could mate immediately by R or Q–R8.

The object of the following maneuver is to open the KR file.

1. **RxP**　　**KxR**

Forced.

2. **R–R1 ch**　**K–Kt1**
3. **R–R8** mate.

Mate No. 9A

White to play and mate in 3

The presence of a Black Bishop, able to defend Black's Kt2 and R1, does not always stop the attack.

Mate No. 9

White to play and mate in 3

Mate No. 9B

White to play and mate in 2

In mate 9A it is necessary to open the KR file. Thus:

1. RxP   B—Kt2

And now a sacrifice will get rid of the Bishop:

2. R—R8 ch ! BxR
3. RxB mate.

The maneuver is almost the same in mate 9B:

1. R—R8 ch   BxR
2. RxB mate.

Mayet's Mate

If, in the bargain, Black's BP is pinned, White is able to open the file still more rapidly:

Mate No. 9C

White to play and mate in 2

1. QxP ch   PxQ
2. R—R8 mate.

Lolli (1763) has demonstrated that even a Black Queen, in spite of its superiority over the Bishop, cannot prevent the mate. The next diagram will show how this may happen. The mating device partakes of both mates 8A and 9.

G. LOLLI

Jean-Baptiste Lolli, born at Modena, was a first-rate player and the author of a very well-known treatise on Chess.

White to play and mate in 5

1. Q—R6   Q—B1

The only move.

2. QxRP ch   KxQ
3. R—R1 ch   Q—R3

Or 3. . . . K—Kt1; 4. R—R8 mate.

4. RxQ ch   KxR
5. R—R1 mate.

Because the White Bishop controls not only White's Kt7 and R8 but also Kt5.

And here is the final aspect of mate No. 9:

Pattern of mate No. 9

Black is mated

It does not matter if Black's Knight's Pawn is missing; and the Bishop might be anywhere on the long diagonal except Kt7 or R8.

Mates of the type 8 and 9 are the ones most frequently met in practice, and examples are certainly not lacking.

GAME NO. 61

French Defense

Berlin Tournament, September 16, 1881

	BLACKBURNE	SCHWARTZ
1.	P—K4	P—K3
2.	P—Q4	P—Q4
3.	Kt—QB3	Kt—KB3
4.	PxP	PxP
5.	Kt—B3	B—Q3
6.	B—Q3	P—B3

7.	O—O	O—O
8.	Kt—K2	B—KKt5
9.	Kt—Kt3	Q—B2
10.	B—K3	QKt—Q2

To get some initiative, White deliberately allows the doubling of his Pawns on the KB file. White also obtains the open KKt file.

11.	Q—Q2	KR—K1
12.	QR—K1	Kt—K5
13.	Q—B1	QBxKt

By these exchanges, Black hopes to reach a position where he will be able to give perpetual check.

14.	PxB	KtxKt
15.	RPxKt	BxP
16.	K—Kt2	

This move came as a surprise to Schwartz, who expected 16. PxB, QxP ch, etc., with perpetual check. By refusing the sacrifice, White gets control of the KR file. In spite of appearances, his King is quite safe.

16.	. . .	B—Q3
17.	R—R1	Kt—B1

Black, compelled to defend his KR Pawn, plays his Knight to B1 in preference to B3, since on the former square it also controls his Kt3.

18. R—R3

Grouping his forces for an attack. The text move practically compels Black to weaken his castled position by advancing one of the defending Pawns.

18. ....   P—KKt3

After Black's 18th move

This is a typical position. Black's castled position is weak, with two holes on his B3 and R3. White has full control of the KR file; Black is demoralized by his failure to obtain a draw and plays weak moves. But even if he had found the best moves, he would sooner or later have succumbed to White's attack, since the latter has two Bishops, two Rooks and the Queen pointed at Black's castled position. On the other hand, however weak White's castled po-

sition may seem, it has only two Black Pieces pointed at it, which will not even be available for attacking purposes. Furthermore, Black does not even have an open file on the King's wing.

19. QR—R1   QR—Q1 ?

A purposeless move. Better would have been 19. . . . B—K2, trying to bring this Bishop to Kt2 via B3 in order to defend the King's position.

20. B—KKt5   R—Q2 ?
21. P—QB4

The plan of bringing the Bishop to B6, followed eventually by RxP, would be refuted by . . . B—R7! The idea of the text move is to play P—B5, followed by B—KB4, B—K5 and eventually by a Rook sacrifice.

21. . . .   PxP
22. BxP   P—KR4 ?

Because White was threatening B—B6, followed by Q—R6. However, the text move weakens the castled position still further.

23. R—R4 !

Preventing 23. . . . B—B5 and also preparing 24. B—B6.

| 23. . . . | P—Kt4 |
| 24. B—Q3 | Kt—K3 ? |

It is a mistake to shift the Knight from its defensive position.

25. B—B6

By the text move we come to one of our typical mating positions. The threat is not only 26. Q—R6 but also 26. RxP, PxR; 27. RxP, followed by 28. R—R8 mate (mate No. 9).

25. . . . Kt—Kt2 is not sufficient because of 26. Q—R6, B—B1; 27. RxP, and mate follows next move.

| 25. . . . . | Kt—B5 ch |

Everything seems to be all right, for the Knight not only checks the King but also controls Black's vital KR4. This position is famous and is present in almost every Chess book. The following sacrifices have been universally admired and praised. The reader who has become familiar with mate No. 9 should easily find Blackburne's reply.

| 26. QxKt ! ! | BxQ |
| 27. RxP | resigns. |

Mate is absolutely inevitable, e.g., 27. . . . PxR; 28.

RxP, B—R3; 29. RxB, Q—R7 ch; 30. KxQ and 31. R—R8 mate.

After Black's 25th move

GAME NO. 62

Réti's Opening

Played at Rotterdam in 1923

M. EUWE	R. LOMAN
1. Kt—KB3	P—Q4
2. P—B4	P—Q5
3. P—QKt4	P—KKt3
4. B—Kt2	B—Kt2
5. Kt—R3	

The object of this rather odd-looking move is to attack the stray Pawn by 6. Kt—B2.

| 5. . . . | P—K4 |

These two Pawns look fairly safe now, but on account of their premature advance they will become an easy target for White later on.

| 6. Kt—B2 | B—Kt5 |
| 7. P—K3 ! | Kt—K2 |

If 7. . . . P—K5; 8. P—
KR3, and if 7. . . . P—Q6; 8.
Kt—R3, followed by 9. Q—
Kt3.

| 8. PxP | PxP |
| 9. P—KR3 | BxKt |

Forced in order not to lose a
Pawn.

10. QxB	P—QB3
11. P—KR4	O—O
12. P—R5	R—K1
13. O—O—O	P—R4

This reaction comes too late
in the day.

14. RPxP	KRPxP
15. Q—KR3	PxP
16. KtxQP !	

This Knight cannot be captured . . .

| 16. . . . | BxKt ? ? |

. . . but Black falls right
into the trap. White mates in
two.

After Black's 16th move

| 17. Q—R8 ch ! | BxQ |
| 18. RxB mate. | |

This is the typical position
of mate No. 9B.

END-GAME NO. 17

*Magdeburg Tournament, July,
1927*

SPIELMANN   L'HERMET

White plays and mates in 5

1. QxRP !

Threatens 2. QxP mate
(mate No. 7) and also 2. Q—
R7 ch, followed by 3. Q—R8
mate (corridor mate).

| 1. . . . | PxQ |
| 2. PxP dis ch | K—B1 |

It would be premature now
to play 3. P—R7, threatening
4. P—R8 = Q mate (mate No.
8), since Black need only shift
his Queen to give a flight
square to the King. Therefore:

3. R—Kt8 ch !	KxR
4. P—R7 ch	K—B1
5. P—R8 = Q mate.	

GAME NO. 63

Vienna Game

Manchester Tournament, 1900

E. SCHALLOP   GOSSIP

1. P—K4	P—K4
2. Kt—QB3	Kt—KB3
3. P—B4	P—Q4
4. BPxP	KtxP
5. Kt—B3	KtxKt

This move favors White's development, and for this reason modern players will play 5. . . . B—K2.

6. KtPxKt	B—K2
7. P—Q4	O—O
8. B—Q3	B—KKt5
9. R—QKt1	P—QKt3
10. O—O	P—QB4
11. P—KR3	B—R4

After Black's 11th move

This position calls for the Greco sacrifice:

12. BxP ch	KxB
13. Kt—Kt5 ch	BxKt
14. QxB ch	

Here there followed 14. . . . . B—R3 and after 15. BxB, PxB; 16. R—B6, Black resigned because of 16. . . . . K—Kt2; 17. QxP ch, K—Kt1; 18. Q—Kt5 ch, K *ad lib.*; 19. R—R6 mate.

Let us, however, examine a better continuation for Black which would have needed more skill and imagination on White's part.

| 14. . . . | K—Kt1 |
| 15. BxB | Q—B2 |

After Black's 15th move

Black is only one Pawn down, and it seems that, in spite of his backward development, he will be able to ward off the attack. But White forces the win by:

16. B—B6 !

And there is no sufficient defense against 17. Q—Kt5, followed by 18. QxP mate (mate No. 8). If 16. . . . P—Kt3; 17. Q—R8 mate. There is no defense. For instance:

(A)

16. . . .	R—QB1
17. Q—Kt5	K—B1
18. QxP ch	K—K1
19. Q—Kt8 ch	K—Q2
20. QxP ch	K—B3
21. Q—K6 ch	K—Kt2
22. QxQP ch	

And it is just a matter of technique to bring the game to a victorious conclusion.

(B)

The other continuation leads to disaster even more rapidly, e.g.:

16. . . .	PxB
17. KPxP	Q—Kt6

The only move which prevents 18. Q—Kt5 ch, followed by mate.

18. R—B5 !

And Black can resign. If the Black Knight joins the defense, then:

(C)

16. . . .	Kt—Q2
17. Q—Kt5	KtxB

18. PxKt	P—Kt3
19. Q—R6, etc.	

GAME NO. 64

French Defense

A. NIMZOVITCH   X.

(*Remove White's QKt*)

A well-known variation of the French defense also leads to the Bishop sacrifice.

1. P—K4	P—K3
2. P—Q4	P—Q4
3. P—K5	P—QB4
4. Q—Kt4	Kt—QB3
5. Kt—KB3	PxP
6. B—Q3	KKt—K2
7. O—O	Kt—Kt3
8. R—K1	B—K2
9. P—QR3	O—O
10. P—KR4	

After White's 10th move

10. . . .   KtxRP

This capture seems a very safe move, since White does not control the KR file.

11.	BxP ch !	KxB
12.	Kt—Kt5 ch	BxKt
13.	BxB	Q—B2
14.	QxKt ch	K—Kt1

After Black's 14th move

| 15. | B—B6 ! | KtxP |
| 16. | RxKt ! | QxP |

If 16. . . . PxB; 17. QKt3 ch, etc.

| 17. | R—Kt5 | Q—Kt3 |
| 18. | RxQ and wins. | |

And if after 15. B—B6 !, PxB; 16. PxP, and mate No. 8 follows.

END-GAME NO. 18

After many moves in a game (Pillsbury–Wolf, Monte Carlo Tournament, 1903) the following position arose from a strictly orthodox defense of the Queen's gambit declined.

Monte Carlo Tournament, November, 1903

H. N. PILLSBURY   H. WOLF

After White's 15th move

This game had developed according to the pattern made famous by the Pillsbury–Tarrasch game (Hastings, 1895). Black is aiming for an end-game, when he will be able to make use of his Queen's side Pawn majority. White, on the other hand, is striving for a decisive attack on the castled position.

Here Pillsbury was able to build up what is known as the "Pillsbury formation," characterized by a Knight on his K5, supported by a Pawn on his KB4 and, if possible, the Rook is brought to KR3 via B3.

In the diagram shown above, White has just played 15. R—R3.

| 15. . . . | P—Kt3 |

The first result—White has

forced the weakening of Black's castled position.

16. **B—Kt1   KtxKt**

In such a position many players lose their self-control and exchange the very troublesome Knight, notwithstanding the fact that by so doing, White's BP occupies a very threatening position and the KB file is open for still more pressure on the castled position. It was suggested that the best move, here, would be: 16. ... Kt—B1, defending his KR2. Certainly not 16. ... B—KB1; 17. KtxKt, losing a Piece.

17. **BPxKt   Kt—Q2**

17. ... Kt—K5 was necessary; but Black underrates the strength of the White offensive and is playing for a counterattack on the Queen's wing.

18. **BxB   RxB**

As will be seen, this double exchange in no way relieves the pressure.

19. **Q—B3   Kt—B1**
20. **R—B1   Q—Q2**
21. **Q—B6**

The Queen is on a square which is usually occupied by a Bishop or a Pawn. It is imperative for Black to drive it away.

21. ....   **P—Kt5?**

A very weak move indeed—first of all, because it is pointless to think of a superior endgame when a mating attack is being hatched on the other side of the board; secondly, the text move is a first-rate tactical blunder, for it enables the Knight to join the attack.

22. **Kt—R4!   Q—B2**

And not 22. ... R—K3; 23. Q—B2, QxKt; 24. QxP ch, with a winning attack.

23. **Kt—B5   B—B1**
24. **R—R6   P—R4**

Still the same golden dream: the counterattack on the Queen's side.

25. **R—B4   R—Kt1**

With the idea of playing ... R—Kt3, dislodging the Queen, but this move comes too late.

White's next move is the winning one, and the reader should be able to find it for himself, without looking at the text, if he remembers the typical mating maneuvers we have just studied.

26. BxP !

After Black's 25th move

This move exploits the weakness of Black's first rank. If 26. . . . BPxB, QxKt mate. It also threatens mate in four if Black were to play an indifferent move. For instance:

26. . . .	P—B6
27. BxRP ch	KtxB
28. RxKt	KxR
29. R—R4 ch	K—Kt1
30. R or Q Kt8 mate	
(mate No. 9).	

Or else:

26. . . .	KtxB
27. RxKt ch	RPxR
28. R—R4	*ad lib.*
29. R or Q—R8	
mate.	

Let us now return to the game:

| 26. . . . | R—Kt3 |

Here Pillsbury missed the

bus. He had two moves which enabled him to mate in five, as was shown by an amateur of Pittsburgh, Pennsylvania, James G. Boyce, namely: 27. P—K6 and 27. Kt—K6. We shall examine one of these continuations at the end of the game.

| 27. QxQR | KtxB |

Or 27. . . . QxQ; 28. BxP ch, KtxB; 29. RxQ, and White, having won the exchange and two Pawns, must easily win the game.

| 28. Q—KB6 | R—K1 |

If 28. . . . KtxR; 29. PxKt, followed by 30. R—R5, and wins.

29. R—B1	B—K3
30. Q—Kt5	K—R1
31. Q—R5	Kt—B1
32. KtxB	RxKt
33. RxR	resigns.

After 33. . . . KtxR; 34. RxP, and wins.

Let us now go back to White's twenty-seventh move and examine the continuation which would have enabled him to carry on the attack he so brilliantly started.

27. Kt—K6 !

Threatening mate by 28. Q–Kt7.

27. . . .	RxKt
28. BxP ch	KtxB
29. R–Kt4 ch	Kt–Kt4
30. RxKt ch	K–B1
31. R–R8 mate.	

Or else:

27. . . .	BxKt
28. BxRP ch	KtxB
29. RxKt	KxR
30. R–R4 ch	K–Kt1
31. R–R8 mate.	

In both cases we have mate No. 9.

GAME NO. 65

Queen's Gambit Accepted

VIENNA VARIATION

Played in August, 1939, on board the Piriapolis, *somewhere between Antwerp and Buenos Aires*

This game was one of the ones played on board the *Piriapolis* among players who were going to take part in the international team tournament of Buenos Aires, August, 1939, while heavy storm clouds were gathering over Europe. To while away the boredom of the long journey, many variations were analyzed, especially those in the Vienna defense, which

derived from a game played in Moscow between Kotoff and Judovitch.

We do not know whether the following game was really played or whether it was just an analysis. The authors are also unknown. But it is a splendid illustration of mate No. 9, and for this reason deserves to be included in our collection of games.

1. P–Q4	P–Q4
2. Kt–KB3	Kt–KB3
3. P–B4	P–K3
4. B–Kt5	PxP
5. P–K4	B–Kt5 ch
6. Kt–B3	P–B4

This is a variation of the Queen's gambit accepted, analyzed by Grünfeld and very popular among Viennese players from 1935 to 1938.

7. BxP

This is an innovation, due to the Russian Grand Master Kotoff in his game against Judovitch. Earlier, one played 7. P–K5 (Fine–Grünfeld, Amsterdam, 1936; Fine–Euwe, A.V.R.O., 1938).

7. . . .	PxP
8. KtxP	Q–R4
9. BxKt !	BxKt ch

Judovitch did not want to

take any risks and played 9.
. . . PxB, leaving White with
a marked advantage.

10. PxB   QxP ch
11. K—B1 !   QxB ch
12. K—Kt1

After White's 12th move

This is an extraordinary position which has been subjected to very many analyses,
which seem to prove that the
only defense for Black is 12.
. . . Kt—Q2!; 13. R—B1,
Q—R3!; 14. BxP, KR—Kt;
15. B—R6, and it is as yet impossible to ascertain which
side is better off.

12. . . .   O—O?
13. Q—Kt4   P—KKt3
14. Q—B4

Threatening Q—R6, fol-
lowed by mate No. 9.

14. . . .   Kt—Q2
15. P—K5   KtxB
16. PxKt

And now there is a Pawn instead on the vital square, and
the threat is mate No. 8.

16. . . .   K—R1
17. R—Q1

Giving additional support to
the Knight, and threatening at
the same time to play P—
KR4—R5, etc.

17. . . .   Q—Kt5
18. Q—R6   R—Kt1
19. Kt—B3 !

Threatening R—Q8.

19. . . .   Q—B1
20. Kt—Kt5 !

After White's 20th move

A very beautiful move, almost problem-like. White
threatens 21. QxP mate, and if
20. . . . QxQ; 21. KtxP mate.
Black thinks that a Rook sacrifice will prove a sufficient defense.

20. . . .   R—Kt2
21. R—Q8 ! !   resigns.

Because now that the Queen is pinned, White threatens 22. QxR mate (No. 8) and if 21. . . . R—Kt1, unpinning the Queen, then 22. QxP mate.

"What a splendid game!" said V. Kahn on his return from Buenos Aires.

"I have already seen something like that!" replied G. Renaud, and thereupon he placed the Pieces as in the following diagram.

END-GAME NO. 19

C. M. DE LABOURDONNAIS, 1833

White to play and mate in 9

Here is the solution of the problem:

1. Q—R6   R—Kt1
2. Kt—K4   Q—KB1
3. Kt—Kt5 !   R—Kt2

Up to now the theme is the same as in the last game. But the continuation is different because of the difference in material.

4. Kt(1)—B3   K—Kt1
5. Kt—K5   K—R1
6. Kt—Q7   Q—KKt1
7. P—R3   Q—KB1
8. KtxQ   K—Kt1
9. QxR mate.

These attacks may also occur against an uncastled King, as in the next example.

END-GAME NO. 20

New Jersey Tournament, 1895

LISSNER   J. S. LOYD

After Black's 22nd move

In this position, Black has just played . . . R—Kt5. This move gives White the opportunity of a Queen sacrifice, as he will have time to double the Rooks on the Q file, threatening mate, while Black is busy capturing the Queen.

23. RxB   RxQ
24. QR—Q1

Threatening mate in two. Black's position is hopeless, and he will have to give back material.

24. . . .   B—K2
25. RxB ch   K—B1

The King has been able to move; but White renews his threat.

26. KR—Q7   K—Kt1
27. R—Q8 ch   resigns.

GAME NO. 66

Caro–Kann

Vienna, February, 1929

R. SPIELMANN   B. HOENLINGER

1. P—K4   P—QB3
2. P—Q4   P—Q4
3. Kt—QB3   PxP
4. KtxP   Kt—KB3
5. Kt—Kt3   P—K3
6. Kt—B3   P—B4

Black's fifth move has blocked the Queen's Bishop and the text move intends to liberate it after P—QKt3.

7. B—Q3   Kt—B3

More accurate would have been . . . PxP, followed by . . . B—Q2 and . . . Kt—B3.

8. PxP   BxP
9. P—QR3   O—O
10. O—O   P—QKt3
11. P—Kt4   B—K2
12. B—Kt2   Q—B2

This is a waste of time and gives White a better position. The right move is 12. . . . B—Kt2.

13. P—Kt5

Known for his attacking style, Spielmann has already taken measure of his young opponent, and he does not mind weakening his Queen's wing to obtain the initiative on the opposite side. On the other hand, the attacked Knight hasn't much choice. On its R4 it would be practically out of play and . . . Kt—Kt1 would permit B—K5.

13. . . .   Kt—R4
14. Kt—K5   B—Kt2
15. Kt—Kt4!   Q—Q1

Black now recognizes how unsound his twelfth move was. White threatens KtxKt ch, smashing the castled position. 15. . . . KtxKt would have been obviously bad; but 15. . . . Q—KB5 should be considered. The continuation might have been 16. BxKt, BxB; 17. Kt—R5, Q—Kt4; 18.

Kt(5)xB, PxKt; 19. P—KB4, with an attack.

   16. Kt—K3   Kt—Q4?

After Black's 16th move

This is another mistake; this Knight was necessary for the defense of the castled King. With five Pieces aiming at the Black King, White is methodically starting a decisive attack. First of all, he is going to weaken the Black King's position by forcing a Pawn advance.

   17. Q—R5   P—Kt3

Black is absolutely resourceless. 17. . . . KKt—B3 loses a Piece, e.g., 18. BxKt, P—Kt3; 19. BxB, etc. On 17. . . . P—B4, Spielmann himself showed the following continuation:

   17. . . .   P—B4
   18. Kt(K3)xP   PxKt
   19. KtxP

And now White threatens mate in four: 20. KtxB ch, Q or KtxKt; 21. BxP ch, K—R1; 22. B—Kt6 dis ch, K—Kt1; 23. Q—R7 mate. The student can see for himself that 19. . . . Kt—B3 and 19. . . . R—B3 are also unsatisfactory. Mate cannot be avoided, even at the cost of a heavy loss in material. If 17. . . . P—KR3, then another sacrifice becomes possible, e.g.,

   17. . . .   P—KR3
   18. BxP !   KxB

Insufficient would be 18. . . . Kt—Kt4, not on account of BxR (which in itself is enough to win the game), but 19. QxP, etc.

   19. Kt(K3)xB5 ch   PxKt
   20. KtxP ch   K—B3
   21. QxP ch   K—K4
   22. P—B4 ch

with a withering attack.

It seems impossible for a player, even for a master like Spielmann, to foresee all the consequences, including the sacrifices, which his move 17. Q—R5 might entail. But one must remember that all these tactical complications are not really so important. The fundamental fact about such a position is that an experienced player feels almost instinctively that five Pieces, concentrated against the Black King's weak position, must bring the game to a successful conclusion. Whatever defense is tried, there comes a stage where a decisive sacrifice is possible, leading either to an inevitable mate, or to such loss of material as to compel the opponent to resign.

The text move brings about another weakening, and enables Spielmann to end the game brilliantly.

18. Kt—Kt4!   B—KB3

Not 18. . . . PxQ; 19. Kt—R6 mate. This is mate No. 19B, which we shall study later on.

18. . . . Kt—KB3 is no better. For instance: 19. Q—K5, and the Knight, three times attacked, cannot withdraw on account of 20. Q—Kt7 or R8 mate. So 19. . . . K—Kt2; 20. Kt—R5 ch!, PxKt; 21. Q—Kt5 ch, K—R1; 22. KtxKt, and wins. Or 19. . . . Q—Q4; 20. QxQ, BxQ (if 20. KtxQ; 21. Kt—R6 mate); 21. KtxKt ch, winning a Piece. And finally, if 18. . . . P—B3; 19. BxKtP,

PxB; 20. QxP ch, K—R1; 21. Kt—R5, and wins. The text move, therefore, seems the best defense, though still not sufficient.

19. KtxB ch   KtxKt

If 19. . . . QxB; 20. BxQ, PxQ; 21. KtxP, and Black has lost a Pawn with the prospect of an utterly hopeless endgame:

20. Q—R6   R—B1
21. QR—Q1   Q—K2
22. KR—K1   Kt—K1

The only square on which it defends its Kt2. The decisive moment has arrived. Now White has six Pieces concentrated against the Black King.

After Black's 22nd move

23. Kt—B5!   Q—B4

What else could be done in that unpleasant position? If 23. . . . KtPxKt; 24. BxP, P—

B3; 25. BxP ch, K—R1, and White forces the win by 26. BxR or 27. R—Q7.

If 23. ... Q—B2; 24. B—B6!, and Black will have to give up his Queen to avoid being mated by 25. Kt—K7, since it is impossible to play 24. ... KtPxKt; 25. R—K3! or 24. ... KPxKt; 25. RxKt.

24. R—K5	B—Q4

After the text move, Spielmann announced mate in four.

25. Kt—K7 ch	QxKt
26. QxRP ch !	KxQ
27. R—R5 ch	K—Kt1
28. R—R8 mate.	

Yielding the pattern of mate No. 9.

CHAPTER 11: *Anderssen's Mate*

(VARIATION OF NO. 9)

We have already seen how the KKt's Pawn's advance of one square weakens the castled position. It is therefore obvious that the weakness would be still greater were this Pawn to advance two squares; likewise, if this Pawn has been exchanged, or captured, or doubled on a neighboring file. The reason for this is that yet another diagonal has been opened to the action of a hostile Bishop, viz., the King's

Bishop. This will give White the opportunity for a new kind of sacrifice in order to open the Rook's file.

1. BxP ch   KxB
2. Q—R5 ch   K—Kt1
3. Q—R8 mate.

The next diagram shows the same type of mate, except that the KKt's Pawn is absent. 1. Q—Kt2 ch would not lead to mate because the Black Knight or Bishop can cover the check.

Mate No. 9D

White to play and mate in 3

Mate No. 9E

White to play and mate in 3

1. BxP ch	KxB	1. BxP ch	KxB
2. Q—R5 ch	K—Kt1	2. R—R1 ch	K—Kt1
3. Q—R8 mate.		3. R—R8 mate.	

The main characteristic of this diagram is the presence of White's Bishop on B6, or elsewhere on the same long diagonal, commanding the squares Kt7 (mate No. 7) and R8 (mate No. 9). The opening of the R file by a Rook sacrifice (mate No. 9), or by a Bishop sacrifice (mates Nos. 9D and E), or by a Queen sacrifice (mates Nos. 9C and F) allows a heavy Piece to mate on R8.

If there were a Pawn on Kt7 instead of a Bishop on B6, mate No. 7 would become impossible, but it would still be possible to consummate all forms of mates No. 9.

Mate No. 9F

White to play and mate in 3

And here are a few practical examples of Anderssen's mate:

END-GAME NO. 21

London Tournament, 1886

I. GUNSBERG   SCHALLOP

After White's 23rd move

In this game, having already sacrificed two Pawns, Black obtained an early initiative. White has just played 23. R—K1, attacking Black's Rook for the second time. Schallop, instead of protecting the Rook, played a move which compelled his opponent to resign. Before looking at the text, try to find it, bearing in mind mate No. 9D.

23. . . .	Q—KB3 ! !
24. resigns.	

There is no defense against the threat. If, for instance, 24. RxR, B—R7 ch; 25. KxB, Qx RP ch; 26. K—Kt1, Q—R8 mate.

The next game is an example of mate No. 9E, delivered at an early stage of the game.

GAME NO. 67

French Defense

Played in Denmark, 1934

K. BLOM   V. JENSEN

1.	P—K4	P—K3
2.	P—Q4	P—Q4
3.	Kt—QB3	PxP
4.	KtxP	B—Q3
5.	B—Q3	Kt—K2
6.	B—KKt5	O—O ?

A fatal error. Before castling, Black should have obtained control of his KB3 by . . . Kt—Q2.

After Black's 6th move

This game is hopelessly lost for Black. There are four White Pieces ready to undertake a swift attack against the King's position. Moreover, not only does the King's Knight intercept the Queen's diagonal, but it does not even fulfill its essential defensive function— to cover its KR2.

7. Kt—B6 ch ! !

The idea of this sacrifice is to unmask the K Bishop's diagonal, smashing the castled position if it is accepted, and if not, attacking Black's KR2 twice.

7. . . .   PxKt

The refusal of the sacrifice would have led to the following continuation:

7.	. . .	K—R1
8.	Q—R5	P—KR3
9.	BxP	Kt—B4

If . . . PxB; 10. QxP mate. If . . . PxKt; 10. B—Q2 dis ch, followed by 11. Q—R7 mate.

If . . . P—KKt3; 10. Q—R4, Kt—B4; 11. BxKt, and mate in three follows. If . . . Kt—Kt1; 10. B—Kt5 ch, Kt—R3; 11. BxKt, P—Kt3; 12. Q—R4, and mate can only be de-

layed by heavy and useless sacrifices.

10.	BxP double ch	KxB
11.	Q—Kt5 ch	K—R1
12.	BxKt	B—Kt5 ch
13.	K—B1	QxKt
14.	Q—R5 ch!	Q—R3
15.	QxQ ch	K—Kt1
16.	Q—R7 mate.	

We have given these varia-
tions in order to show that
Black was irredeemably lost.
Now let us go back to the text:

    8. BxBP!

We have now reached the
typical positions of diagram
9D and diagram 9E. Mate can
only be avoided at the cost of
the Queen.

    8. . . .   Q—Q2

Black has only taken into
account the vertical check and
unpins the Knight in order to
cover it.

9.	BxP ch	KxB
10.	Q—R5 ch	K—Kt1
11.	Q—R8 mate.	

END-GAME NO. 22

Barmen, 1869

ANDERSSEN   ZUKERTORT

White to play and mate in 5

Here is another combination
based on mate No. 9—prob-
ably its prototype.

| 29. | QxP ch | KxQ |
| 30. | P—B6 dis ch | |

To prevent the action of the
Black Queen on this rank.

30.	. . .	K—Kt1
31.	B—R7 ch	KxB
32.	R—R3 ch	K—Kt1
33.	R—R8 mate.	

This combination of Anderssen's is practically in every
Chess book. It always makes a
great impression on those who
judge the value of a combination by the value of the sacrificed Pieces.

CHAPTER 12: *Pillsbury's Mate*

(NO. 10)

The power of the double check, which we have already studied, is sometimes made use of to bring about typical mates, especially the Rook and Bishop mate (as in mate No. 9).

The next diagram shows a position which is often met in practice, but which is usually very badly handled by amateurs.

Mate No. 10

White to play and mate in 3

The first move is fairly obvious:

1. RxP ch	K—R1
2. R—Kt8 double ch	

This double check will enable White to force mate.

2. . . .	KxR
3. R—Kt1 mate.	

Pattern of mate No. 10

Black is mated

There is no shortage of practical examples. Here are two of them:

END-GAME NO. 23

Riga, 1899

A. S. STEPANOW   X.

1. RxP ch	K—R1
2. R—Kt8 double ch	KxR

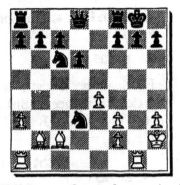

White to play and mate in 4

3. R—Kt1 ch   Q—Kt4
4. RxQ mate.

The next position is somewhat more complicated, and the typical mate is hidden. The main thing is not to let it slip by.

END-GAME NO. 24

White to play and mate in 6 or wins a Piece

1. BxKt   RxQ
If . . . BxB; 2. QxB, P—

Kt3; 3. Kt—B3, and White is a Piece up.

2. RxP ch   K—R1
3. R—Kt8 double ch   KxR
4. R—Kt1 ch   R—Kt5
5. RxR ch   Q—Kt4
6. RxQ mate.

Pillsbury's Mate (or Mate No. 10B)

In this mate again there is an elementary application of the double check. In the next diagram some beginners, no doubt, would capture the Rook and be content with the exchange. An experienced player, however, would prefer to announce mate in three.

White to play and mate in 3

1. R—Kt1 ch   K—R1
2. B—Kt7 ch   K—Kt1
3. BxP dis ch mate.

The final aspect of this mate is the same as mate No. 10.

The following game will show this mate in an amusing way:

GAME NO. 68

Queen's Gambit Declined

London, 1899

H. N. PILLSBURY   **LEE**

1.	P—Q4	P—Q4
2.	P—QB4	P—K3
3.	Kt—QB3	Kt—KB3
4.	B—Kt5	QKt—Q2
5.	P—K3	B—K2
6.	Kt—KB3	P—QKt3 ?

This move, which has never been considered very good in the orthodox defense of the Queen's gambit, is particularly bad before castling. It was Pillsbury himself who found a brilliant refutation.

7. PxP

Since Black has shown his intention of developing his Queen's Bishop on the long diagonal, White starts by forcing him to block this diagonal.

7. . . .   PxP

Black cannot succeed in keeping this diagonal open by capturing with the Knight, e.g., 7. . . . KtxP; 8. KtxKt,

BxB; 9. KtxP ch, and he loses a Pawn.

8. B—Kt5

Pinning the Knight and threatening to place his Bishop in the hole which Black has made (B6).

8. . . .   B—Kt2
9. Kt—K5 !

Attacking the pinned Knight for the second time, and also controlling once more Black's weak QB3.

9. . . .   O—O
10. B—B6   R—Kt1

If 10. . . . BxB; 11. KtxB, Q—K1; 12. KtxB ch, as in the game.

11.	BxB	RxB
12.	Kt—B6	Q—K1
13.	KtxB ch	QxKt

This is the whole point of the maneuver. Black must lose a Pawn.

14. KtxP   Q—K5

Attacking at the same time the Knight and the KKt Pawn.

15.	KtxKt ch	PxKt
16.	B—R6	QxKtP

This is a blunder which, however, is excusable for a

player who is not familiar with typical mating positions.

After Black's 16th move

It seems a very good move because it not only wins back the Pawn, but also attacks an unsupported Rook. There is, however, a winning move for White.

17. Q—B3 !

This is one of the finest Queen sacrifices on record. If it is accepted, White mates in four, thus:

17. . . .	QxQ
18. R—Kt1 ch	K—R1
19. B—Kt7 ch	K—Kt1
20. BxP dis ch	Queen covers
21. RxQ mate.	

Giving a typical instance of mate No. 10B. Black resigned on his seventeenth move, since a refusal of the sacrifice would have cost him a Rook.

END-GAME NO. 25

J. OWEN   X.

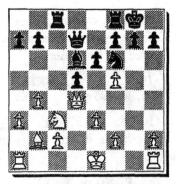

After Black's 14th move

White has a magnificent position. By shifting the Knight, he can completely dominate the long diagonal, and he also has an open file for his Rook.

15. KtxP !

It is obvious that Black cannot play . . . KtxKt on account of 16. QxP mate. He has, however, three plausible continuations: 15. . . . PxKt or 15. . . . Kt—K1, which, as we shall see, lead to mate, and 15. . . . P—K4; 16. KtxKt ch, with a material advantage for White.

15. . . .   PxKt

And White announces mate in three.

16. QxKt   PxQ
17. R—Kt1 ch K—R1
18. BxP mate.

Let us now turn to the other defense, which was actually played in the game.

15. . . .   Kt—K1
16. Kt—B6 ch !   PxKt

If 16. . . . KtxKt; 17. Qx Kt, etc., as in the last variation.

17. R—Kt1 ch K—R1

If 17. . . . Kt—Kt2; 18. Rx Kt ch, etc.

After Black's 15th move

18. QxP ch   KtxQ
19. BxKt mate.

And both variations end with mate No. 10.

CHAPTER 13: Quízzes

EXERCISE NO. 29

Paris, 1903

J. TAUBENHAUS   D. JANOWSKI

White played 31. Q–QB1. Is
this move good?

EXERCISE NO. 30

*Simultaneous Display
Holland, 1931*

A. ALEKHINE   A. VAN MIDENO

White to play and mate in 5

EXERCISE NO. 31

Warsaw, 1917

A. RUBINSTEIN   BELSITZMANN

Black to play and mate in 3

EXERCISE NO. 32

Le Havre, 1939

R.   R. DANIEL

Black to play and mate in 5

EXERCISE NO. 33

ANDERSSEN   X.

White to play and mate in 4

EXERCISE NO. 34

Carlsbad, 1907

R. TEICHMANN   J. MIESES

Black to play. Is there a threat?
If so, how can he meet it?

EXERCISE NO. 35

NEUMANN   J. DUFRESNE

White to play and mate in 3

EXERCISE NO. 36

Carlsbad, 1907

M. VIDMAR   R. TEICHMANN

Why doesn't Black play 26.
. . . QxP?

EXERCISE NO. 37

Correspondence Tournament, 1914

G. COURTEAUD   A. SEMINARIO

Black to play and mate in 5

EXERCISE NO. 38

Zurich Tournament, 1934

W. HENNEBERGER   BERNSTEIN

White played 1. Q—Kt4 and the game was a draw. Was there a better move?

EXERCISE NO. 39

San Remo Tournament, 1930

BOGOLJUBOFF   MONTICELLI

Black to play and mate in 4

EXERCISE NO. 40

KLIEFOTH   SCHLIEMANN

White to play and mate in 9

CHAPTER 14: *Damiano's Mate*

(NOS. 11, 12, 13)

The study of mate No. 8 has led us to the conclusion that a Pawn, placed on B6 and controlling Kt7, becomes extremely strong and enables a player to force many different mates.

This conclusion also applies to other Pawn positions. This gives us the opportunity to examine other types of mate which derive from them. In the following diagram, a White Pawn is on White's Kt6 and allows White to mate in three.

Mate No. 11A

White to play and mate in 3

    1. Q—R5   R anywhere
    2. Q—R7 ch   K—B1
    3. Q—R8 mate.

This mate only becomes possible if Black's K2 is obstructed. In 1512, Damiano

published the following amusing position, in which White must get rid of his cumbersome Rooks to be able to mate with the Queen.

END-GAME NO. 26

P. DAMIANO, 1512

White to play and mate in 5

1. R—R8 ch	KxR
2. R—R1 ch	K—Kt1
3. R—R8 ch	KxR
4. Q—R1 ch	K—Kt1
5. Q—R7 mate.	

If there had been no Black Rook, and the Black Queen had been on its K2, after 5. ... K—B1, White would have mated by 5. Q—R8 mate. This mating pattern is the same as mate No. 8.

When there is no Black Pawn in front of the King, White can deliver another type of mate, provided he can check on his first move.

Mate No. 11B

White to play and mate in 3

1. Q—R5 ch	K—Kt1
2. Q—R7 ch	K—B1
3. Q—B7 mate.	

A very common maneuver, similar to Damiano's, consists in removing a Black Piece which might block the way from R7 to B7.

Mate No. 11C

White to play and mate in 3

1. R—R8 ch	BxR
2. Q—R7 ch	K—B1
3. Q—B7 mate.	

This mating device holds good for any file, as the next piquant mate will show.

END-GAME NO. 27

International Team Tournament, Hamburg, 1930

L. BETBEDER   TYROLER

White to play and mate in 3

1. R—B8 ch   BxR
2. Q—B7 ch   K—Q1
3. Q—Q7 mate.

END-GAME NO. 28

New York Tournament, 1889

J. S. BLACKBURNE   LIPSCHÜTZ

White to play

Both players have the same number of Pieces, but Black has two very strong past Pawns, which give him excellent chances in the end-game. As it is, however, one does not see any marked advantage for White. The Queen and the Rook are on a closed file, the Knight is not very aggressively placed, and the only two Pieces which look as if they mean business are the Queen's Rook and the Knight's Pawn. But it is precisely this Pawn, solidly supported, which to the experienced player has a very

important significance. It allows the Queen to mate on its R7. But how can the Queen reach this square? The answer is already included in the question, and Blackburne did not hesitate.

1. RxP ch   KxR

The sacrifice must be accepted; if not, there is an immediate forced win, e.g., 1. . . . K—R1; 2. R—R7 ch, K—Kt1; 3. P—Kt7!, and Black is lost if 3. . . . KxR; 4. P—Kt8 = Q ch, RxQ; 5. QxR mate. Or 3. . . . R(1)—B3; 4. R—R8 ch, K—B2; 5. P—Kt8 = Q ch, and mate follows in two moves. Or 3. . . . R—Q1; 4. R—R8 ch, and mate in three moves. Finally, if 3. . . . K—B2; 4. P—Kt8 = Q ch, and mate next move.

2. Kt—R5 ch !

The idea of this move is to open White's diagonal R2—Kt8.

2. . . .   RxKt

The nonacceptance of the sacrifice does not change things, e.g., 2. . . . K—Kt1; 3. Q—B7, R(4)—B2; 4. PxR double ch, K—R2; 5. Q—Kt3!,

B—Kt5; 6. QxB, and mate next move.

3. Q—B7 ch resigns.

The Black King cannot return to his first rank on account of Damiano's mate, 4. Q—R7 mate. And if 3. . . . K—B3; 4. Q—Q6 ch, B—K3 (4. . . . K—Kt2; 5. Q—K7 ch, and mate in two); 5. QxR ch, B—B2; 6. QxB mate.

Damiano's Bishop
(MATE NO. 12)

It is evident that, if White has a Bishop instead of a Pawn, the same mating maneuvers are possible, for the added mobility of the Bishop allows other classic attacks which it is important to know, since they are met with in everyday practice.

Mate No. 12A

White to play and mate in 2

1. B—Kt6 dis ch K—Kt1
2. Q—R7 mate.

The pattern is the same as mate No. 8 with a Bishop instead of a Pawn.

Mate No. 12B

White to play and mate in 3

1. B—Kt6 ch King plays
2. Q—R7 ch K—B1
3. QxP mate.

The following position frequently occurs in practice:

Mate No. 12C

White to play and mate in 4

Nine times out of ten, the beginner will play QxP ch, and be surprised afterward to find that the King is able to escape after all. This position is similar to the ones we have just studied, and the same mating maneuver must be applied. The correct moves are:

1. BxP ch   K—R1
2. B—Kt6 ch   K—Kt1
3. Q—R7 ch   K—B1
4. QxP mate.

The stratagem, which consists in getting rid of a Rook to give the Queen a free passage, is also applicable to this type of position.

Mate No. 12D

White to play and mate in 5

1. BxP ch   K—R1
2. B—Kt6 dis ch

In order to block the Black Queen.

2. . . .   K—Kt1
3. R—R8 ch   KxR
4. Q—R5 ch   K—Kt1
5. Q—R7 mate.

This maneuver is frequently met in practice, as the next diagram illustrates.

N. MAXIMOW   X.

White to play and mate in 5

1. B—R7 ch   K—R1
2. B—Kt6 dis ch   K—Kt1
3. R—R8 ch   KxR
4. Q—R5 ch   K—Kt1
5. Q—R7 mate.

Mate No. 13

We have already met several types of mate in which a pin played an important part (2A, 8B, 8C, 9C). The simplest type is the one given by a Queen supported by a Bishop (the shepherd's mate), first introduced by Damiano in 1512.

END-GAME NO. 29

P. DAMIANO, 1512   *Mate No. 13*

White to play and mate in 2   *White to play and mate in 3*

    1. QxP ch   K—Kt1
    2. QxP mate.

A Rook sacrifice on the first move will bring about Damiano's position.

    1. R—R8 ch   KxR
    2. Q—R6 ch   K—Kt1
    3. QxP mate.

CHAPTER 15: *Morphy's Mate*

(NOS. 14, 15, 16)

In a game against L. Paulsen at the New York tournament Morphy astonished the onlookers by sacrificing his Queen for a Knight to obtain a mating attack. This has become a classic sacrifice.

Mate No. 14A

White to play and mate in 3

1. QxKt   PxQ

The acceptance of the sacrifice, which in this case is forced, opens both a file and a diagonal for White.

2. R—Kt1 ch   K—R1
3. BxP mate.

The final position of this mate is very similar to the one of mate No. 10.

Pattern of mate No. 14A

Black is mated

Mate No. 14B

White to play, mates in 3 or wins a Piece

The same mate takes place if the King has not yet castled, and if the Rook is on its initial square, provided White controls the King's file.

1. QxKt   PxQ
2. B—R6 ch   K—Kt1
3. R—Kt1 mate.

In this case the mate pattern is very much the same as mate No. 10.

Pattern of mate No. 14B

Black is mated

If Black's first rank were not defended by a Rook, White could also mate by R—K8.

As can easily be seen, this last pattern is just a variation of the corridor mate.

In practice it is rare to obtain a position where mate follows in a given number of moves after a Queen sacrifice; usually Morphy's sacrifice gives

a winning attack, culminating in mate, only to be delayed by counter-sacrifices. The above game, however, is a very typical example of mate No. 14B, delivered in a given number of moves.

Pattern of mate No. 14C

Breslau, 1876

RIEMANN   ANDERSSEN

Black to play and mate in 5

1. . . .   QxKt ch
2. PxQ   B—R6 ch
3. K—B2   B—R5 ch
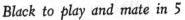

4. K—Kt1   R—K8 ch
5. Q—B1   RxQ mate.

Mates Nos. 15 and 16

Before examining the famous Paulsen–Morphy game, let us study mates Nos. 15 and 16.

Mate No. 15

White to play and mate in 2

If there were no Rook on Black's B1, there would be an immediate mate; therefore, the object of the maneuver will be to get rid of the Rook by means of a sacrifice.

1. QxR ch   KxQ
2. R—K8 mate.

This type of mate is a variation of the corridor mate No. 1. The same kind of mate can occur without the doubling of the Rooks, e.g.,

1. QxR ch   KxQ

2. B—B5 ch   K—Kt1
3. R—K8 mate.

Mate No. 15A

White to play and mate in 3

The first move eliminates the Rook, the second one forces the King in the corridor and the third one delivers mate. We have not given these mates in Chapter I (second part) because the mating maneuver is quite different. The

Mate No. 16

White to play and mate in 3

next diagram will show how this mate can also occur diagonally.

1. QxR ch   KxQ
2. B—R6 ch   K—Kt1
3. R—K8 mate.

And now a practical example:

END-GAME NO. 31

F. VON BARDELEBEN   X.

White to play and mate in 3

1. QxR ch   KxQ
2. B—B6 ch   K—K8
3. R—B8 mate.

Morphy's Sacrifice

GAME NO. 69

Four Knights' Opening

New York International Tournament, November, 1857

L. PAULSEN   P. MORPHY

1. P—K4   P—K4
2. Kt—KB3   Kt—QB3

3. Kt—B3   Kt—B3
4. B—Kt5   B—B4

A modern player would prefer the symmetrical move 4. . . . B—Kt5 or Rubinstein's defense 4. . . . Kt—Q5.

5. O—O

5. KtxP would have given White a slight advantage.

5. . . .   O—O
6. KtxP   R—K1

After 6. . . . KtxKt; 7. P—Q4, White recaptures the Piece with a better development.

7. KtxKt

A positional mistake to play the same Piece three times, giving Black the better development.

7. . . .   QPxKt
8. B—B4   P—QKt4

Black cannot, as yet, win back the Pawn. For instance: 8. . . . KtxP; 9. KtxKt, RxKt; 10. BxP ch, KxB; 11. Q—B3 ch, winning the exchange. The text move forces White to decide whether he will play B—Kt3, allowing . . . B—KKt5 or B—K2, abandoning the pressure on Black's KB Pawn.

9. B—K2   KtxP
10. KtxKt

A very weak move would have been 10. B−B3, enabling Black to force the win as follows: 10. . . . KtxBP; 11. Rx Kt, Q−Q5; 12. Kt−K4 (and not 12. Q−B1, QxR ch; 13. QxQ, R−K8 mate), 12. . . . RxKt; 13. BxR, QxR ch; 14. K−R1, B−KKt5; 15. B−B3, R−K1, forcing mate.

10. . . .	RxKt
11. B−B3	R−K3
12. P−B3 ?	

This is a bad blunder, since it causes a fatal weakening of his Q3. Black will immediately seize this square and paralyze the Queen's wing. Much better would have been 12. P−Q3, with, at least, an equal game, for Black's superior development offers no compensation for his doubled Pawn.

12. . . .	Q−Q6

Simple and effective, since White is now compelled to develop his Queen's wing artificially.

13. P−QKt4	B−Kt3
14. P−QR4	PxP
15. QxP	B−Q2

This is not the best move because it abandons his R3 to the White Queen. 15. . . .

B−Kt2 is the right move, and the game might have continued 16. R−R2, QR−K1 (threatening 17. . . . QxR ch, followed by 18. . . . R−K8 mate); 17. Q−Q1, B−R3 !

16. R−R2 ?

A decisive mistake. Paulsen was probably not aware of his opponent's intentions and was about to play 17. B−R3.

16. . . .	QR−K1

Threatening . . . QxR, followed by mate (mate No. 15).

17. Q−R6

After White's 17th move

With the text move, White parries the threat but enables Black to place a Queen sacrifice still worthy of admiration. After 17. Q−Q1, P−QB4 would follow 18. . . . B−Kt4.

17. . . .	QxB !

The idea of this sacrifice is to open the Knight's file and diagonal; on account of the inactivity of the White Queen, of the Q's Bishop and the Q's Rook, this sacrifice is absolutely decisive. It is said that the spectators of this game, who were very average players, did not understand the import of this sacrifice and thought that Morphy had suddenly gone mad.

18. PxQ   R—Kt3 ch
19. K—R1   B—R6

Threatening 20. .... B—Kt7 ch; 21. K—Kt1, BxP mate. There is no real effective defense against this threat, if, for instance, 20. R—Kt1, RxR ch; 21. KxR, R—K8 mate. If 20. Q—Q3 (attacking the Rook), P—KB4; 21. Q—B4 ch, K—B1 !, and White must play 22. R—Q1 as in the game.

20. R—Q1

Here Morphy could have mated in six, but he missed the strongest continuation.

20. ...   B—Kt7 ch
21. K—Kt1   BxP dis ch
22. K—B1

And the game went on 22. ... B—Kt7 ch; 23. K—Kt1,

B—R6 dis ch (the text move also wins, but a more elegant conclusion would have been: 23. .... B—K5 ch; 24. K—B1, B—KB4 !; 25. Q—K2, B—R6 ch; 26. K—K1, R—Kt8 mate); 24. K—R1, BxP; 25. Q—B1, BxQ; 26. RxB, R—K7; 27. R—R1, R—R3; 28. P—Q4 ?, B—K6, and White resigned.

After White's 20th move

Here is the strongest continuation:

22. ...   R—Kt7
23. Q—Q3 !

If 23. QxB, RxRP; followed by R—R8 mate.

23. ...   RxP ch
24. K—Kt1   R—Kt7 double ch
25. King plays R—Kt8 mate.

Since this memorable game, Morphy's sacrifice has been repeated many times.

In Morphy's Footsteps

GAME NO. 70

MacDonnell Gambit

Played in London, 1869

G. MACDON- S. BODEN
NELL, JR.

 1. P—K4 P—K4
 2. B—B4 B—B4
 3. P—QKt4?

A very doubtful gambit, which was very popular, however, three-quarters of a century ago.

 3. . . . BxP
 4. P—QB3 B—B4
 5. P—Q4 PxP
 6. PxP

Probably a developing move, such as Kt—KB3, would have been much better.

 6. . . . B—Kt5 ch
 7. K—B1

This move demonstrates the absurdity of the opening selected. White gives up castling in order to proceed with an attack which cannot prove successful. The idea is to play 8. Q—Kt3. If 7. B—Q2, BxB ch; 8. KtxB, Kt—KB3; 9. P—K5, P—Q4, and Black has an extra Pawn and a good position. In an open game, no

opening will allow White (if Black plays correctly) to hold the center permanently and to keep two Pawns there.

 7. . . . B—R4?

A very silly move, for the Bishop is quite as unprotected on its R4. The right move here is 7. . . . Q—K2.

 8. Q—R5?

A mistake seems to call forth another mistake. 8. BxP ch, KxB; 9. Q—R5 ch, followed by QxB would have enabled White to regain his Pawn and to equalize, but apparently White does not want equality, he wants an attack!

 8. . . . P—Q4
 9. BxP

Here also, it would have been preferable to play 9. PxP, and if . . . Kt—KB3, then 10. Q—K2 ch.

 9. . . . Q—K2
 10. B—R3 Kt—KB3 !
 11. BxP ch QxB
 12. QxB Kt—B3 !
 13. Q—R4 KtxKP

Let us now survey the situation. So far, the material is the same on both sides, but not so the position; White

cannot castle; he has only two
Pieces in action and he has
lost his Pawn center. Black,
with two tempi ahead and a
better position, should win.

14. Kt—KB3	B—Q2
15. QKt—Q2	KtxKt ch
16. KtxKt	O—O—O !
17. QR—Kt1	

If 17. Kt—B3, KtxP; 18. Qx
Kt, B—Kt4 ch, and wins the
Queen. However, better would
be 17. K—Kt1.

17. . . .	Q—Q4 !
18. Kt—B3	B—B4
19. R—Q1	KR—K1
20. B—B5 ?	

Black's last move was a prep-
aration for the following sacrifice which White has completely overlooked, since he
was only thinking of protecting his QR Pawn.

After White's 20th move

20. . . .	QxKt ! !
21. PxQ	B—R6 ch
22. K—Kt1	R—K3
23. Q—B2	

To prevent mate by QxR if
. . . R—Kt3 ch.

23. . . .   RxP !

A brilliant move, threatening . . . RxR, followed by
. . . R—Kt3 mate. Also good
would have been 23. . . . .
Kt—K4; 24. Q—K4, R—Kt3
ch; 25. QxR, KtxP mate.

| 24. BxR | KtxB |
| 25. resigns. | |

White cannot defend simultaneously his K1 (mate by the
Rook), his Kt6 (mate by the
Rook) and his B3 and K2
(mate by the Knight). In this
game as in the last one, the
Queen sacrifice does not immediately lead to mate but to
a winning attack.

Here is a more recent ex-
ample:

GAME NO. 71

Center Gambit

Copenhagen, 1918

KIRDETZOFF   V. KAHN

| 1. P—K4 | P—K4 |
| 2. P—Q4 | PxP |

3. QxP	Kt—QB3
4. Q—Q1	Kt—B3
5. Kt—QB3	B—Kt5
6. B—Q3	O—O
7. B—KKt5	R—K1

It is clear that because of White's weak opening, Black already has the initiative.

| 8. Kt—B3 | KtxP ! |

This elegant move can hardly be called a Queen sacrifice, for after 9. BxQ, KtxKt dis ch; 10. K—B1, KtxQ, Black regains the Queen with an extra Piece.

| 9. BxKt ! | BxKt ch |

Necessary in order to avoid the loss of a Piece.

10. K—B1	B—B3
11. BxB	QxB
12. Q—Q3	

The skirmish is over and Black has won a Pawn and has the advantage. In view of the following combination he gives up the KR Pawn.

| 12. . . . | Kt—Kt5 |
| 13. Q—B4 | P—Q4 ! |

The Queen's Bishop's diagonal is thereby opened without loss of time.

14. BxP ch	KxB
15. QxKt	P—B4
16. QxBP ?	

White falls into the trap. If 16. Q—R4 ch, QxQ; 17. Ktx Q, B—Q2, threatening . . . B—Kt4 ch, followed by . . . R—K7.

| 16. . . . | QxKt ! ! |

Morphy's sacrifice!

After Black's 16th move

17. PxQ	B—R6 ch
18. K—Kt1	R—K3
19. Q—B7	

Parrying the threat R—Kt3 mate, but 19. Q—Q4, R—Kt3 ch; 20. Q—Kt4 would have been better.

| 19. . . . | QR—K1 |
| 20. R—KB1 | |

The only move.

| 20. . . . | R—K8 ! |
| 21. resigns. | |

Marshall has played Morphy's sacrifice several times

during his career. At Saint Sebastian, 1911, it enabled him to draw in an unfavorable position. This diagram shows how he used it brilliantly against Janowski in his third match game.

END-GAME NO. 32

Third Match Game, Biarritz, 1912

D. JANOWSKI   F. J. MARSHALL

After White's 12th move

This position results from the Petroff defense. White has played the opening rather carelessly and cannot castle, but as a compensation he has a strong center and can start an attack on the Black castled position by BxP ch. But the surprise is yet to come.

12. . . .   QxKt !
13. PxB

White cannot accept the sacrifice on account of 13. PxQ, B—R6 ch; 14. K—Kt1, R—K8 ch; 15. B—B1, RxB mate. The text move, nevertheless, is not sufficient. It might have been better to drive away the Queen by P—KR3, but even in this case, White would have lost a Pawn.

13. . . .   Kt—B3 !

Threatening to win a Pawn. The Queen, in the meantime, is still immune.

14. B—Kt2   KtxKtP !
15. BxP ch   K—R1
16. PxQ   B—R6 ch
17. K—Kt1   KtxQ
18. BxKt

Scorning danger, as was often the case with Janowski, a very aggressive player, he wins a Piece; but as the master Goetz says in his *Cours d'Echecs*: "A mere glance at the following diagram will convince the reader how heavily this Piece is being paid for. The position cannot be held much longer and Marshall ends the game magnificently."

Black has a double advantage: a positional one, for the

White King is absolutely im-
mobilized, and a material one,
because White's K Rook is out
of action and restricting the
King's freedom.

After White's 18th move

In view of this, there seem
to be two methods of attack
for Black: firstly, a check on
the open file; secondly, doubling the Rooks on the King's
file with a swift mate.

18. . . .   R—K7

This is the first double attack because it threatens one
of the Bishops and also prepares the doubling of the
Rooks with a strong mating
threat.

19. R—QB1   QR—K1
20. B—B3

White's two last moves
were forced and Black's posi-

tion is so strong that there are
several winning moves.

After White's 20th move

In our opinion, the best
continuation at this juncture
would have been: 20. . . . R
xB !; 21. RxR (if 21. R—K1,
RxR ch; 22. BxR, R—B8; 23.
ad lib., RxB mate); R—K3;
22. B—Q2, R—Kt3 ch; 23. B—
Kt5, RxB mate (mate No.
14B).

20. . . .   R(1)—K6 !
21. B—Kt4 ?

Bad, but in any case the position is hopeless, e.g., 21. P
xR, R—Kt7 ch; 22. K—B1, R
xB dis ch; 23. K moves, RxR
ch, followed by . . . RxR,
and Black, with a Rook up,
must win. Or 21. B—K4, Rx
QB; 22. R—Q1, R(6)—K6;
23. R—B1, R—K8; 24. B—Q3,

RxR ch; 25. BxR, R—K8, and mate follows.

21. . . .   R(6)xP
22. B—Q1   R—B3
23. resigns.

Mate is inevitable. The Paulsen–Morphy game has shown us the sacrifice in a primitive form, although the game was not concluded in the best possible manner.

Twelve years later, the Mac-Donnell–Boden game repeated the pattern in a more elaborate form with a problem-like conclusion.

Finally, the Kirdetzoff–Kahn and Janowski–Marshall games both utilized the possibility of a vertical and horizontal mate, exploiting the open KKt file and the weakness of White's first rank.

CHAPTER 16: Quizzes

EXERCISE NO. 41

Played in France, at the end of the nineteenth century

L. GUINET   X.

White to play and mate in 4

EXERCISE NO. 42

X.   GAUDERMEN

Black to play and mate in 4

EXERCISE NO. 43

(*Without the Q's Kt*)

S. WINAWER   X.

White to play and mate in 4

EXERCISE NO. 44

New York, 1924

A. ALEKHINE   FREEMAN

White to play and mate in 4

EXERCISE NO. 45
United States, 1850

RICHARDSON   DELMAR

White to play and mate in 4

EXERCISE NO. 46

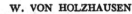
W. VON HOLZHAUSEN   X.

White to play and mate in 5

EXERCISE NO. 47
Buffalo, 1893

POLLOCK   ALLIES

White to play and mate in 5

EXERCISE NO. 48
Prague Chess Club, 1913

J. NEUMANN   G. BERGMANN

White to play and win

EXERCISE NO. 49

Malvern Tournament, 1921

F. D. YATES   SIR G. THOMAS

Black to play and win

EXERCISE NO. 50

A. F. MACKENZIE   X.

White to play and mate in 3

EXERCISE NO. 51

Kiev Tournament, 1944

D. BRONSTEIN   V. GOLDENOV

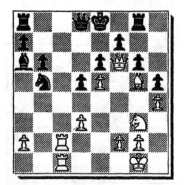

White to play and mate in 3

EXERCISE NO. 52

Helsingfors Tournament, 1936
(Modified Position)

P. KÉRÉS   T. GAUFFIN

*White to play and win a
Piece or to mate in 3*

CHAPTER 17: *Mate with Heavy Pieces*

(NOS. 17 AND 18)

In 1512, P. Damiano published the following position, which shows another typical sacrifice. The idea is to open a file by sacrificing a heavy Piece, allowing another heavy Piece to mate.

END-GAME NO. 33

Mate No. 17A

P. DAMIANO, 1512

White to play and mate in 3

1. QxP ch   KxQ
2. R—R2 ch   Q—R5
3. RxQ mate.

The following diagram is the mate pattern:

Pattern of mate No. 17

Black is mated

Here is a practical example:

END-GAME NO. 34

Played in a simultaneous blind-fold display on eight boards, December 18, 1932

A. ALEKHINE   BOROCHOW

20. Q—R5 ch   K—Kt1
21. KtxP !   R—B1
22. R—Kt4   K—R1
23. R—K3   P—K4
24. Kt—K6 !

Black resigned. In fact, if he had taken the Knight he

After Black's 19th move

would have fallen into Damiano's position:

24. . . .   BxKt

After Black's 24th move

25. QxP ch   KxQ
26. R—R3 ch   B—R5
27. R(3)xB mate.

It is usually in a slightly different manner that this mate is met with in practice, viz.:

1. Q—Kt4 ch   K—R1
2. RxP ch   KxR
3. R—R1 mate.

Mate No. 17B

White to play and mate in 3

Let us note that the association of Queen and Rook has an enormous mating power. In the following diagram Black possesses all his Pieces and, in spite of that, the Black King will be relentlessly driven by the White Queen and Rook to the mating square.

White to play and mate in 6

1. Q—Q7 ch   K—K4
2. R—B5 ch   K—K5

3. Q–Q5 ch	K–K6
4. R–B3 ch	K–K7
5. Q–Q3 ch	K–K8
6. R–B1 mate.	

The logical conclusion is that all sacrifices are permissible which expose the opponent's King to the crossfire of the Queen and Rook.

Here is another typical mate often met in practice:

Mate No. 17C

White to play and mate in 4

1. RxP ch

A Rook sacrifice forces the typical position. The nonacceptance of the sacrifice would lead to 2. QxP mate.

1. . . .	KxR
2. QxP ch	K–R1 or R3

The second Rook now becomes active. In many practical cases the attacking side must prepare the mate by a quiet move (castles Queen or K–K2) to make way for the second Rook.

3. R–R1 ch	Q–R6
4. RxQ mate.	

Pattern of mate No. 17C

Black is mated

And now, let us turn to some practical examples of mate No. 17. The next in-

St. Petersburg, 1905

M. N. KATALYMOV   A. BAZAROV

After White's 17th move

stance is typical. Black succeeds in mating with reduced material (Queen and two Rooks).

17. . . .   RxP ch
18. K—R1

If 18. KxR, R—Kt1 ch, followed by 19. Q—B6 or Q—R3 mate.

18. . . .   RxP ch
19. KxR

If 19. K—Kt1, R—Kt1 ch and mate next move.

19. . . .   Q—R5 ch
20. K—Kt2   Q—Kt5 ch

Taking control of his B6 and thus preventing the King's flight.

21. K—R2   Q—R4 ch
22. K—Kt2   R—Kt1 mate.

GAME NO. 72

Scotch Opening
Nice, 1941

G. R.   N. N.

1. P—K4   P—K4
2. Kt—KB3   Kt—QB3
3. P—Q4   PxP
4. B—QB4   B—K2

This timid move seeks to avoid the complications as-sociated with 4. . . . Kt—B3 and 4. . . . B—B4.

5. KtxP   KtxKt

Not to be recommended, because it speeds up White's development.

6. QxKt   Kt—B3
7. Kt—B3   P—Q3
8. B—KKt5

Better than 8. castles. White must prepare to castle on the Queen's side, as he has control of the Queen's file and his Queen is on its Q4.

8. . . .   P—KR3

A useless precaution which only weakens the Pawn structure.

9. B—R4   B—K3
10. O—O—O

White's advantage is evident; with the exception of the King's Rook, all his Pieces are already in action. Black, on the other hand, has no good continuation on account of the passive position of his King's Bishop and of the time he wasted exchanging Knights.

10. . . .   BxB

After the text move, White will be able to launch an immediate attack.

11. QxB   O—O
12. P—K5 !

It is in the interest of the player with the better development to open files; in this case it is all the easier as Black's Queen's Pawn is pinned.

12. . . .   Kt—Q2
13. BxB   QxB

A bad move would have been 13. . . . KtxP; 14. BxQ, KtxQ; 15. BxP, etc.

14. PxP   PxP
15. Q—Q5

The most effective continuation, since Black's isolated Queen's Pawn is doomed. Black, however, tries to complicate the game.

15. . . .   Kt—Kt3
16. QxQP

White has now won a Pawn as the result of his better development. Black's wisest course is to exchange Queens with fair drawing chances. Instead of that, he prefers to counterattack.

16. . . .   Q—Kt4 ch
17. P—B4

Covering the check and starting a King's side attack.

17. . . .   QxKtP ?

Despair or presumption? He regains the Pawn but opens a file against his own King.

18. KR—Kt1

Taking immediate control of the file, and now Black is threatened with QxP.

18. . . .   Q—B7

The capture of the Rook's Pawn would lead to a very quick defeat, e.g., 18. . . . Q xRP; 19. Q—B6 !, P—Kt3; 20. R—R1, and there is no defense against 21. RxP, followed by 22. R—R8 mate, unless Black is willing to sacrifice a Piece (20. . . . Kt—Q2; 21. Q—Q6 .or Q4 !, etc.).

19. QxP   Q—K6 ch
20. K—Kt1   P—Kt3

*After Black's 21st move
White mates in 7*

21. QR–K1
21. . . .   Q–Q7 ? ?
22. RxP ch   PxR
23. QxP ch   K–R1
24. Q–R5 ch   K–Kt2
25. R–Kt1 ch   Q–Kt7
26. RxQ ch   K–B3
27. Q–K5 ch   K–B2
28. R–Kt7 mate.

Even after 21. . . . Q–Q5, controlling its Kt8 and preventing mate, Black has no adequate defense. For instance: 22. P–B5, Q–Kt2; 23. Q–Kt5 !, and White threatens P–B6 or Kt–B6 via K4. If 23. . . . P–B3, White would be left with two extra Pawns and a very strong position.

This powerful Queen and Rook attack can also occur against an uncastled King. In the last two examples we have seen how a Rook was sacrificed in order to smash the castled position and to bring the King within the field of action of the Queen and Rook. In the next famous Morphy game White sacrifices two Knights and a Rook to draw the King into the center of the board, where the Queen and Rook are waiting to force mate.

GAME NO. 73

Two Knights' Defense

Played in 1858 in New Orleans in a blindfold display on six boards.

P. MORPHY   N. O.

1. P–K4   P–K4
2. Kt–KB3   Kt–QB3
3. B–B4   Kt–B3
4. P–Q4   PxP
5. Kt–Kt5

Until recently, this move was judged premature and 5. castles was preferred.

5. . . .   P–Q4 !
6. PxP   KtxP ?

This is a wrong move and it is strange that in this opening such a small inaccuracy should lose the game. The right answer is 6. . . . Kt–K4, recommended by Jae-

After White's 7th move

nisch, which seems to leave Black with a slight advantage.

7. O—O

There is no satisfactory defense for Black. White threatens to play 8. KtxBP, KxKt; 9. Q—B3 ch, etc.

7. . . .   B—K2

This seems a good move. It attacks the Knight, prepares for castling, and covers an eventual Rook check. But Morphy refutes this defense brilliantly.

8. KtxBP!   KxKt
9. Q—B3 ch   K—K3

On any other move, White recaptures the sacrificed Piece with his Bishop and has the better position. The whole game proves convincingly that the King must not come to the center of the board to try to keep the extra Piece.

10. Kt—B3!

A second sacrifice which is still more decisive than the equally winning move 10. R—K1 ch.

10. . . .   PxKt
11. R—K1 ch   Kt—K4

The reader will be able to find out for himself how the retreat of the King either leads to mate or to the loss of the Queen.

12. B—B4   B—B3
13. QBxKt   BxB
14. RxB ch!

The third sacrifice.

14. . . .   KxR

All Black's moves are forced and the King is being drawn toward the center.

15. R—K1 ch   K—Q5

The only way of avoiding mate in two.

After Black's 15th move

This is one of the finest examples of the mating power of Queen and Rook.

16. BxKt!

Black is defenseless. For instance: if 16. . . . QxB; 17. QxP mate.

16. . . .   R—K1

Here Morphy announced mate in seven.

17. Q—Q3 ch   K—B4
18. P—Kt4 ch   KxP !

If 18. . . . K—Q3; 19. B—B3 mate. If 18. . . . K—Kt3; 19. Q—Q4 ch, and mate in two follows.

19. Q—Q4 ch   K—R4
20. QxP ch   K—R5
21. Q—Kt3 ch   K—R4
22. Q—R3 ch   K—Kt4
23. R—Kt1 mate.

"Yes, but what if I had played PxP on my sixteenth move?" asked Morphy's opponent at the conclusion of the game.

"Mate in six," said Morphy simply, his back still turned to the boards.

16. . . .   PxP
17. R—K4 ch K—B4
18. Q—R3 ch KxB
19. Q—Q3 ch K—B4
20. R—B4 ch K—Kt4
21. Q—Kt3 ch K—R4
22. R—R4 mate.

We shall now give a more recent game ending with mate No. 17:

GAME NO. 74

Slav Defense

U. S. A. Championship, New York, 1944

A. S. DENKER   H. V. KLEIN

1. Kt—KB3   P—K3
2. P—Q4   P—Q4
3. P—B4   P—QB3
4. P—K3   Kt—Q2

The continuation 4. . . . Kt—B3 is more accurate, and if White plays 5. QKt—Q2, then 5. . . . P—QB4, followed by . . . Kt—B3.

5. Kt—B3   KKt—B3
6. B—Q3   B—Q3
7. O—O   O—O
8. P—K4   PxKP

Tchigorin's continuation, 8. . . . PxBP !; 9. BxP, P—K4, seems more accurate.

9. KtxP   KtxKt
10. BxKt   P—KR3

A timid move. Much more enterprising would have been 10. . . . P—QB4.

11. R—K1   Kt—B3
12. B—B2   R—K1
13. P—QKt3   B—Kt5
14. B—Q2   BxB
15. QxB   Q—Q3
16. QR—Q1   R—Q1
17. Q—K3   B—Q2

Black seems to remember at last that he has a Queen's Bishop.

18. Kt—K5   B—K1
19. P—B4

White has a splendid position and a very easy game, as every move increases his pressure on the opponent.

19. . . .   Q—B2
20. P—KKt4 !   Kt—Q2
21. Q—Q3

Threatening 22. Q—R7 ch, K—B1; 23. Q—R8 ch, K—K2; 24. QxKtP.

21. . . .   Kt—B1
22. P—Kt5

The logical sequel to White's 20th move.

22. . . .   PxP
23. PxP   R—Q3
24. R—K4   QR—Q1
25. R—R4   Kt—Kt3

After Black's 27th move

Parrying the threat Q—R3.

26. KtxKt   PxKt
27. R—KB1 !   RxP

We have now reached a typical mating position.

28. R—R8 ch !   resigns.

Mate cannot be avoided, e.g.:

28. . . .   KxR
29. R—B8 ch   K—R2
30. Q—R3 ch   R—R5
31. QxR mate.

This is one of the typical mates No. 17.

Mate No. 18

The two Rooks (or Rook and Queen), in co-operation with an advanced Pawn, can give a particular form of mate, provided the King's neighboring files are open to attack.

Mate No. 18

White to play and mate in 2

1. R—Kt8 ch

The object of this sacrifice is to force the King into a mating network.

1. . . .   KxR
2. R—K8 mate.

If one looks at the final position of this mate it is easy to see that it is a variation of the corridor mate.

Pattern of mate No. 18

Black is mated

This mate, as in the case of the corridor mate, can take a slightly different form:

White to play and mate in 3

1. QxR ch   KxQ
2. R—B8 ch   Q—Q1
3. RxQ mate.

This is again the corridor mate and the maneuver partakes of mate No. 15A and mate No. 18.

In practice this mate occurs when the attacking side has a Rook on an open file and is able to place a Pawn on his Kt6. Here is a practical example:

END-GAME NO. 36
Berlin, April, 1859
C. MAYET   A. ANDERSSEN

Black to play and mate in 5

11. . . .   BxP ch
12. RxB   Q—Q8 ch
13. Q—K1   QxQ ch
14. R—B1   R—R8 ch
15. KxR   QxR mate.

CHAPTER 18: *Mate by Minor Pieces*

(NO. 19)

A Bishop and a Knight can deliver mate in a corner position, provided the King is blocked by its own Pieces, as the next two diagrams will show.

Pattern of mate No. 19A

Black is mated

Pattern of mate No. 19B

Black is mated

Of course, in these diagrams the Knight could be on its K7 instead of its R6; and in 19B

the Bishop could be anywhere on the diagonal and could also be replaced by the Queen.

These mates can be forced with a Queen sacrifice as in the next example.

Mate No. 19B

White to play and mate in 2

1. Q—R6 !

Threatening mate and forcing the answer.

1. . . .   PxQ
2. KtxP mate.

The Queen sacrifice has forced open the long diagonal and made the Bishop and Knight mate possible.

The next diagram will show how the mere threat of this mate may gain an important tempo.

White to play and mate in 2

Threatening mate.

1. . . .   PxR

The only move, but this capture has opened the fatal diagonal.

2. Q—B6 mate.

Yielding the pattern of mate No. 19A.

Here are a few examples which show that a Queen sacrifice, forcing one of the mates No. 19, has often been applied in practice.

White to play

1. Kt—Kt4 !

And Black cannot capture the Queen on account of:

1. . . .   PxQ
2. Kt—R6 mate.

END-GAME NO. 37

This is a rather artificial example, but it is important to know it since it is taken from an opening variation of the Ruy Lopez.

1. R—KR5 !

END-GAME NO. 38

Paris, 1913

A. AURBACH   X.

In a handicap game, Aurbach obtained this position and set the following trap:

1. B—K3   QxKtP ?

White to play

The amateur took the Pawn without the slightest hesitation. This is the mistake which Aurbach was relying on.

2. B—Q4

This does not seem a very dangerous move; it threatens the exchange, but, on the other hand, leaves the K Bishop *en prise*.

2. . . .   **QxKB**

If 2. . . . Kt—B5, attacking the Queen, 3. KtxB ch, R xKt; 4. QxP mate.

3. Q—R6 !

The Queen cannot be captured on account of mate No. 19B.

3. . . .   **B—KB3**
4. **BxB**   resigns.

Mate is inevitable. This quiet sacrifice attacks Black's Knight's Pawn three times.

It is curious to note that the two forms of mate No. 19, forced by a Knight sacrifice, are present in an opening variation of the Ruy Lopez:

GAME NO. 75

Ruy Lopez

OPENING VARIATION

1.	P—K4	P—K4
2.	Kt—KB3	Kt—QB3
3.	B—Kt5	P—Q3
4.	P—Q4	B—Q2
5.	Kt—B3	KKt—K2

A strange move, recommended by Steinitz. It is not as good as 5. . . . Kt—B3, as it blocks the K Bishop and delays castling.

6. B—QB4 !

It is a waste of time to maintain this Bishop on its Kt5 and, although the text move does not develop a Piece, it gives an immediate advantage to White as it threatens Kt—KKt5.

6. . . .   **PxP**
7. **KtxP**

Commenting on this variation in one of his lectures, Emanuel Lasker stated that the logical continuation for Black should be . . . P–KKt3, followed by . . . B–Kt2, with a strong pressure on the long diagonal. He added that in his match against Steinitz the latter had never adopted this continuation. The next move will show why this line of play is impossible.

    7. . . .   P–KKt3 ?
    8. B–KKt5

Immediately exploiting the weakness of Black's B3. The text move threatens B–B6 and also pins the K Knight.

    8. . . .   B–Kt2
    9. Kt–Q5 !

This brilliant move is very strong. It threatens 10. Ktx QKt, PxKt; 11. BxKt, Q–Kt1; 12. B–B6!, and White remains with a Piece up.

    9. . . .   BxKt

This move spells Black's doom, although it seems good. However, if 9. . . . KtxKt (Q4); 10. BxKt, Q–B1; 11. B–B6 ! and White has won a Piece.

    10. QxB

After White's 10th move

The tactical threats are 11. QxR ch and also 11. Kt–B6 ch, followed by 12. B–R6 mate. Positionally, the idea is to weaken still further Black's KB3 and KKt3, already poorly defended after the removal of the K Bishop.

    10. . . .   O–O

And not 10. . . . KtxQ; 11. Kt–B6 ch, followed by 12. B–R6 mate (mate No. 19A).

    11. Kt–B6 ch   K–R1

11. . . . K–Kt2 would lead to mate in two: 12. Kt–R5 double ch and 13. Q–Kt7 mate.

    12. Kt–Kt4 dis ch   KtxQ

If 12. . . . P–B3; 13. Qx P ch, RxQ; 14. BxR mate. And if 12. . . . Kt–K4; 13.

B—B6 ch, K—Kt1; *14.* Kt—
R6 mate. And finally, if *12.*
. . . K—Kt1; *13.* Kt—R6
mate.

13. B—B6 ch	K—Kt1
14. Kt—R6 mate.	

Mate No. 19 in its most
typical form.

GAME NO. 76

Nimzovitch Defense

Russia, 1939

E. RABINOVITCH   S. GOGLIDZE

1.	P—Q4	Kt—KB3
2.	P—QB4	P—K3
3.	Kt—QB3	B—Kt5
4.	P—K3	O—O
5.	B—Q3	P—Q4
6.	KKt—K2	PxP
7.	BxBP	P—QR3
8.	O—O	P—B4
9.	P—QR3	BxKt
10.	PxB	Q—K2
11.	B—Q3	P—K4

12.	PxKP	QxP
13.	R—Kt1	Kt—B3
14.	Kt—Kt3	
14.	. . .	P—QKt4

The acceptance of the sacrifice would have been fatal,
e.g., *14.* . . . QxBP; *15.* B—
Kt2, Q—R4; *16.* BxKt, PxB;
17. Q—R5, P—B4; *18.* Q—
Kt5 ch, K—R1; *19.* Q—B6 ch,
K—Kt1; *20.* Kt—R5, and
mate is inevitable.

15. P—QB4 !

Opening the long diagonal
to his Q Bishop.

15.	. . .	PxP
16.	BxP	Q—K2
17.	Q—B3	B—K3
18.	Kt—B5 !	Q—Q2
19.	BxB	QxB

If *19.* . . . PxB; *20.* QxKt,
PxKt; *21.* QxBP, winning a
Pawn.

After White's 14th move

After Black's 22nd move

20. B—Kt2	Kt—K4
21. Q—B4	Kt—Kt3
22. Q—Kt5	Kt—K5
23. Q—R6!	resigns.

Because if 23. . . . PxQ; 24. KtxP mate (mate No. 19B).

GAME NO. 77

Vienna Game

Nice, December, 1940

G. RENAUD   X.

1. P—K4	P—K4
2. Kt—QB3	Kt—KB3
3. P—B4	P—Q4
4. PxKP	KtxP
5. Kt—B3	B—QKt5
6. Q—K2	BxKt
7. KtPxB	P—QB3

The game Spielmann–Vidmar, Semmering, 1926, went on: 7. . . . castles; 8. Q–K3, Kt–B3; 9. B–Q3, with advantage to White.

8. Q—K3	O—O
9. B—Q3	B—B4
10. O—O	Q—Kt3
11. Kt—Q4!	B—Kt3
12. BxKt	BxB
13. P—Q3	B—Kt3
14. P—K6!	Kt—R3
15. P—K7	R—K1
16. B—R3	Q—R4

This attempt to win a Pawn is a dangerous loss of time.

17. B—Q6	QxBP

18. QR—Kt1	P—QB4
19. Kt—B5	P—Kt3?

A logical move which, unfortunately, does not take into consideration the tactical possibilities of the position. The right move is 19. . . . BxKt.

After Black's 20th move

20. B—K5!

There is no defense.

20. . . .	QxBP
21. Q—R6!	resigns.

After 21. . . . PxQ; 22. KtxP mate (mate No. 19B).

In the next example an uncastled King is mated.

GAME NO. 78

Grünfeld Defense

U. S. A., 1944

J. JONES   C. TANASSY, JR.

1. P—Q4	Kt—KB3
2. P—QB4	P—KKt3

3. Kt—QB3	P—Q4
4. PxP	KtxP
5. P—K4	KtxKt
6. PxKt	P—QB4
7. B—QB4	

The idea of the text move is to be able to play Kt—K2 without running the risk of having the Knight pinned by . . . B—Kt5.

7. . . .	B—Kt2
8. Kt—K2	Kt—B3
9. B—K3	PxP
10. PxP	

White has got a fine Pawn center, but experience has taught that such a center cannot always be held permanently.

10. . . .	Q—R4 ch
11. B—Q2	Q—R6
12. QR—Kt1	

Defending indirectly the Queen Pawn, because if 12. . . . KtxP, B—Kt4, and Black loses the Queen.

12. . . .	O—O
13. P—Q5	Kt—K4
14. B—Kt4	

The Black Queen seems irrevocably doomed, but . . .

| 14. . . . | Q—KB6 !! |

A very fine trap.

15. PxQ ??

Unforgivably greedy. After 15. O—O !, QxKP; White has lost a Pawn, but can still put up a good defense.

15. . . .	KtxP ch
16. K—B1	B—R6 mate
	(mate No. 19A).

CHAPTER 19: *The Mate of the Two Bishops*

(NO. 20)

We have already seen how a Bishop and Knight suffice to mate the King in the corner and we shall now see that the same result can be achieved with two Bishops.

Mate No. 20

White to play and mate in 2

One of White's Bishops has full control of a diagonal, and a sacrifice will give the other one full control of the mating diagonal.

1. QxBP !

Threatening 2. QxP mate.

1. . . .   PxQ
2. BxP mate.

Pattern of mate No. 20

Black is mated

This mate is so obvious that in practice it usually appears only as a threat. We have already met it in one of the variations of game No. 75. It may also be brought about if Black's KKt1 is obstructed, as in the following example:

1. QxP   PxQ
2. BxP mate.

The following mate, curiously enough, occurs in the

very center of the board. Here is an opening variation of the Queen's gambit declined in which Black is mated after a blunder.

END-GAME NO. 39

White to play and mate in 2

GAME NO. 79

Queen's Gambit Declined

OPENING VARIATION

1. P—Q4	P—Q4
2. P—QB4	P—K3
3. Kt—KB3	Kt—KB3
4. Kt—B3	P—B4
5. B—Kt5	PxQP
6. KKtxP	P—K4

7. KKt—Kt5	P—QR3 !
8. Q—R4	B—Q2
9. PxP	Kt—B3 ?
10. PxKt	BxP
11. P—K4	PxKt
12. Q—Kt3	P—Kt5
13. Kt—Q5	BxKt
14. PxB	QxP ? ?
15. QxQ	KtxQ

Black has tried very hard to win a Pawn and has succeeded at last, but at the cost of . . .

16. **B—Kt5 mate.**

Black is mated

This position, though obtained in a very artificial manner, is as amusing as it is instructive.

CHAPTER 20: *The Mate of the Two Knights*

(NO. 21)

This type of mate is rare in practice, but is nevertheless met with. One of the authors of this book had the opportunity of achieving it in a correspondence game.

Mate No. 21

White to play and mate in 2

This mate would be immediately possible if White's R6 were free and Black's Kt2 obstructed. A sacrifice achieves both aims:

1. Q—Kt7 ch   KtxQ
2. Kt—R6 mate.

There is a pattern of this mate which is frequently used in Chess problems.

Pattern of mate No. 21

Black is mated

Here is an illustration taken from a game played by Blackburne in a simultaneous exhibition:

END-GAME NO. 40

X.   J. H. BLACKBURNE

Black to play and mate in 2

The solution is obvious:

| 1. ... | Q—Kt7 ch |
| 2. RxQ | Kt—R6 mate. |

This mate may also be attained against an uncastled King, as the next amusing game, played between two American amateurs, will prove.

GAME NO. 80

Center Gambit

Long Beach, California, 1945

J. VAN ESSEN   DUFF

1. P—K4	P—K4
2. P—Q4	PxP
3. QxP	Kt—QB3
4. Q—K3	P—QKt3
5. Kt—QB3	B—B4
6. Q—Kt3	P—Kt3

Black has chosen a bad method of development and his position is already weak.

7. Kt—Q5	P—Q3
8. B—KKt5	P—B3
9. Q—QB3	Kt—K4
10. P—QKt4	PxB
11. PxB	KtPxP
12. Kt—B3 !	Kt—B2

After Black's 12th move

Black's position is already crumbling, and White has three powerfully placed Pieces in action.

13. KtxKtP !

With many threats, the chief one being 14. KtxKt, followed by 15. QxR.

13. ...	KKt—R3
14. B—Kt5 ch !	B—Q2
15. Kt—K6 !	Q—B1
16. Q—B6	Kt—Kt1

The typical position has been reached.

| 17. Q—K7 ch ! | KtxQ |
| 18. Kt—B6 mate. | |

After Black's 16th move

CHAPTER 21: *Bishop and Knight Mate*

(NO. 22)

We have already seen how a Knight and Bishop can mate a cornered King. In this chapter we shall examine a different mating device, reminiscent of mate No. 21.

Mate No. 22A

White to play and mate in 3

1. QxP ch   KtxQ
2. Kt—Kt6 ch   K—Kt1
3. B—Q5 mate.

By introducing a pin, a position is obtained wherein either the Bishop or the Knight can mate.

Pattern of mate No. 22B

Black is mated

Mate No. 22C

White to play and mate in 2

1. Kt—Kt6 ch   K—Kt1
2. B—B4 mate.

179

Mate No. 22D

White to play and mate in 2

1. B—B4 ch   K—R1
2. Kt—Kt6 mate.

Here is a very amusing example of this mate:

GAME NO. 81

Giuoco Piano

New York, 1894

A. ALBIN   SHIPLEY

1. P—K4   P—K4
2. Kt—KB3   Kt—QB3
3. B—B4   B—B4
4. O—O   Kt—B3
5. P—B3   O—O ?
6. P—Q4   PxP
7. PxP   B—Kt3
8. P—Q5

White is exploiting Black's weak fifth move and has obtained a strong and mobile center.

8. . . .   Kt—K2

On 8. . . . Kt—QR4; 9. B—Q3, threatening 10. P—QKt4.

9. P—K5   Kt—K1
10. P—Q6   PxP
11. PxP   Kt—Kt3
12. B—KKt5   Kt—B3
13. Kt—B3   P—KR3
14. Q—Q3 !   PxB
15. QxKt   Kt—R2
16. Kt—Q5 !

A very good move and a trap.

16. . . .   PxQ

In those days an amateur never resisted the temptation of capturing a Queen.

After Black's 16th move

White mates in two:

17. Kt—K7 double ch   K—R1
18. KtxP mate.

Mate No. 22 B.

GAME NO. 82

Scotch Opening

*Played in England in the nine-
teenth century*

X.   H. E. BIRD

1. P—K4	P—K4
2. Kt—KB3	Kt—QB3
3. P—Q4	PxP
4. KtxP	Q—R5
5. Kt—Kt5	B—B4
6. Q—B3	Kt—B3
7. KtxP ch	

A developing move would
have been much better. By
choosing this old Steinitz variation of the Scotch opening,
Black was relying on this
greedy blunder.

7. . . .	K—Q1
8. KtxR	R—K1

Five Pieces in action are
worth the sacrifice of the exchange.

9. B—Q3	KtxP
10. O—O	

White rushes for safety, but
it is too late.

10. . . .	KtxP !
11. RxKt	R—K8 ch
12. B—B1	Kt—Q5
13. QxBP	

After White's 13th move

Better than any explana-
tion, a glance will convince the
reader how Black, with his
formidable position (against
White with his hopeless one),
was able to announce mate in
three:

13. . . .	Kt—K7 ch
14. K—R1	RxB ch
15. RxR	Kt—Kt6 mate.

It is an example of mate
No. 22B (forced by the methods of mate No. 3).

CHAPTER 22: The Arabian Mate

(NO. 23)

Before the reforms introduced in the fifteenth century the only Pieces which moved as they do nowadays were the Rook, the Knight, and the King. For this reason, the earliest mate on record, delivered by the Rook and Knight, is called "the Arabian mate."

Mate No. 23

White to play and mate in 3

1. Kt—B6

There is no real defense against 2. R—R7 mate, and Black can only delay the mate.

1. . . .   R—R2
2. RxR   Knight plays
3. R—R7 mate.

Pattern of mate No. 23

Black is mated

In practice this mate appears usually as a threat. Here, however, is an end-game in which it occurs.

END-GAME NO. 40A

Match, 1933, New York

R. FINE   A. W. DAKE

1. KtxBP ! !   KxKt
2. Kt—K4 ch   K—Kt2
3. R—QB2   Q—R5
4. QxP ch   B—Kt3
5. R—B7 ch   K—Kt1

White to play

If 5. . . . R–Q2; 6. Kt–B3 and wins.

6. QxB ch ! !   PxQ
7. Kt–B6 ch   K–R1
8. R–R7 mate.

CHAPTER 23: *Pay Attention to the Ranks!*

There is a Russian saying: "A wood-pusher overlooks the ranks." This means that inexperienced players think mostly in terms of files; ranks are usually overlooked.

It is true that many typical mates consist in opening files and diagonals, either to give a free passage to the mating Piece, or else to obtain control of one of the King's adjoining squares.

The opening of a rank occurs less often in practice. But this is no reason to neglect a possible threat on a rank. The next two examples show what might happen.

END-GAME NO. 41

Carlsbad, 1907

DURAS   OLLAND

In this position, White moved the threatened Knight to B4.

There was, however, a typi-cal three-move mate. Duras, a strong Chess Master, overlooked it because he wasn't thinking in terms of *ranks*.

White to play and mate in 3

| 1. B—B8 dis ch | B—R4 |
| 2. QxB ch ! | PxQ |

White's sixth rank is now open to the action of his Rook.

    3. R—R6 mate.

This is mate No. 14C.

END-GAME NO. 42

Cassel, 1914

DR. MUNK   X.

White to play and mate in 4

If Black's QKt's Pawn were not there, the Rook could mate in one move. White got rid of it in the following manner:

1. Kt—B7 ch   K—R2
2. QxP ch !   PxQ
3. Kt—Kt5 double ch K—R1
4. R—R7 mate.

CHAPTER 24: Quizzes

EXERCISE NO. 53

Nice, 1937

P. MORRA   N. BOSSOLASCO

White to play and mate in 4

EXERCISE NO. 54

H. N. PILLSBURY   X.

White to play and mate in 4

EXERCISE NO. 55

SHOWALTER   X.

White to play and mate in 3

EXERCISE NO. 56

Breslau, January, 1865

ZUKERTORT   ANDERSSEN

White to play and mate in 2

EXERCISE NO. 57

Bremen, March, 1923

HARTLAUB · · · · · · · · · · WAHLE

(*Without the Q's Kt*)

White to play and win

EXERCISE NO. 58

Leipzig, 1926

C. NORMANN · · · · · · · · · · X.

(*Without the Q's R*)

White to play and win

EXERCISE NO. 59

Régence, September, 1872

MEISELS · · · · · · · · · · CLERC

White to play and mate in 2

EXERCISE NO. 60

Nice, 1946

B. ROMETTI · · · · · · · · · · X.

White to play and mate in 7

EXERCISE NO. 61

,X.   X.

White to play and mate in 5

EXERCISE NO. 62

1908

X.   SCHAPIRO

Black to play and mate in 5

EXERCISE NO. 63

Altona, 1928

MITTELMANN   CLAUSEN

White to play and mate in 6

EXERCISE NO. 64

X.   X.

Black to play and mate in 3

EXERCISE NO. 65

DADIAN DE MINGRELIE   X.

White to play and mate in 3

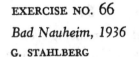

Black to play and win

EXERCISE NO. 67

J. H. BLACKBURNE   X.

White to play and mate in 3

EXERCISE NO. 68

X.   X.

White to play and mate in 3

EXERCISE NO. 69

Carlsbad Tournament, 1907

H. WOLF   A. RUBINSTEIN

EXERCISE NO. 70

Le Havre, 1944

E. V.   R. DANIEL

Black to play and win   *Black to play and mate in 4*

EXERCISE NO. 71

MASON   I. GUNSBERG

EXERCISE NO. 72

Paris Tournament, 1867

S. LOYD   S. ROSENTHAL

White to play and mate in 4   *White to play and mates in 4 or wins a Piece*

EXERCISE NO. 73

Bradford Chess Club, 1913
(Modified Position)

G. SHORIES   X.

White to play and mate in 6

EXERCISE NO. 74

Correspondence Game, 1897–98

K. ZAMBELLY   G. MAROCZY

Black to play and mate in 5

EXERCISE NO. 75

Pistyan Tournament, 1922

R. RÉTI   K. HROMADKA

Black to play and mate in 5

EXERCISE NO. 76

Correspondence Game, 1923

A. J. HEAD   X.

White to play and mate in 6

EXERCISE NO. 77

(*Modified Position*)

A. ALEKHINE   X.

White to play and mate in 6

EXERCISE NO. 78

W. STEINITZ   X.

White to play and mate in 3

EXERCISE NO. 79

(*Modified Position*)

1769

D. L. PONZIANI   X.

White to play and mate in 7

EXERCISE NO. 80

Paris, 1909

M. ZUCKERBAKER   ED. PAPE

Black to play and mate in 7

CHAPTER 25: *In Search of a Typical Mate*

The mere possibility of a mate is not enough in itself to determine your entire strategy and tactics. However, it may suggest certain useful maneuvers. The following examples illustrate this point.

END-GAME NO. 43

International Team Tournament, Folkestone, 1933

C. HAVASI   SACCONI

After Black's 15th move

This position, as any amateur will recognize, arises from the orthodox defense of the Queen's gambit declined.

C. Havasi, a strong attacking player, is about to attack, and starts by exchanging some minor Pieces.

16.	Kt—K5	KtxKt
17.	PxKt	Kt—Q4

With the idea of exchanging as many Pieces as possible.

18.	KtxKt	BxKt
19.	BxKB	BxB

Black, not to lose a Pawn (after 19. . . . RxB; 20. BxB, PxB; 21. RxP) makes a bad move. On account of the Bishops of different colors, he hopes for a draw.

20.	B—R4	Q—Kt2
21.	Q—Kt4	K—R1

Avoiding 22. B—B6.

22. R—Q6

With the intention of doubling the Rooks on this file. Black, however, does not understand the deeper significance of this move.

22. ...   P—Kt5
23. QR—Q1   PxP?

After Black's 23rd move

After all these preparatory maneuvers, White is in a position to launch a very strong attack against the opponent's King. If the reader has followed these maneuvers closely, he will find the winning move without looking at the text.

24. B—B6 ! !   resigns.

White threatens with 25. QxP mate and the only two available defenses (24. ... PxB and 24. ... R—KKt1) are insufficient, e.g.:

First defense:

24. ...   PxB
25. PxP

Repetition of the threat with a Pawn instead of the Bishop (mate No. 8).

25. ...   R—KKt1

The only defense.

26. R—Q8 !

The reason for the doubling of the Rooks: the pin of Black's defense.

26. ...   QRxR
27. RxR

And mate is inevitable. Second defense:

24. ...   R—KKt1
25. QxP ch ! !   RxQ
26. R—Q8 ch   RxR
27. RxR mate.

END-GAME NO. 44

How was it possible, in the following position, to prepare an attack against Black's castled position?

Munich Tournament, 1926

R. SPIELMANN   GEBHARDT

White's position is slightly better, but he has not been able to recover the Pawn which he sacrificed in the opening. A good player could spend hours analyzing the position without discovering its

strength or its weakness. Spielmann saw, in a flash, the continuation which compelled his
opponent to resign on the
sixth move. This is the difference between talent, which is
acquired, and genius, which is
inborn.

After Black's 20th move
Spielmann's plan is to
smash the castled position, exchanging Pieces necessary for
its defense, and also breaking
up the Pawn formation.

21. KtxKt !

A surprising move. White
exchanges his beautifully
placed Knight; but the idea is
to deprive Black of a possible
means of defending his castled position.

21. . . .   QxKt

White's plan is now evident
—first to eliminate Black's

Bishop; secondly, to give his
Q Bishop a larger range of action. Any good player could
formulate this plan, but very
few could carry it out.

22. B—R3 !   Q—B3

Of course not 22. . . . Q
xB on account of 23. BxP ch,
winning the Queen.

23. B—Q5 !

White is not interested in
winning the exchange. He's
after bigger game. Black's
Queen is now compelled to
leave its third rank.

23. . . .   QxBP
24. RxB !

The removal of the Black
Queen justifies this sacrifice.

24. . . .   PxR

White has achieved his
end: the removal of Black's
defenses and the smashing of
Black's Pawn formation. Now
all that remains is to force
mate.

25. Q—Kt3 ch   K—R1
26. B—K7 !   resigns.

White threatens 27. BxP
mate (No. 14A). The continuation might be:

26. ...   Q—B3
27. BxQ   R—KKt1

Black has just resigned

28. BxP ch   R—Kt2
29. QxR mate.

Or else:

27. ...   RxB
28. BxR   B—Kt5
29. QxB   *ad lib.*
30. Q—Kt7 mate.

White's Bishop, which seemed quite out of action, is the Piece which finally delivers mate.

END-GAME NO. 45

Vienna Tournament, 1896

D. JANOWSKI   G. MARCO

White has undertaken an attack on the King's position. For this reason he has opened the KKt's file. Black has brought his Q's Rook to his second rank, and the attack

seems to have reached a stalemate. Janowski's Q's Rook is not yet in action and his problem is to bring it into play without giving Black time to counterattack. A quiet move achieves this result:

22. R—Kt3 !

After Black's 21st move

Black cannot play 22. ...
R—K2 because of 23. Kt—Kt6 ch, PxKt; 24. R—R3 ch, B—R5; 25. RxB mate.

22. ...   BxKt
23. BxB   R—K2
24. Q—R6

The Queen leaves, but for a better position.

24. ...   Q—Q2
25. QR—KKt1

There are now four Pieces attacking Black's Kt2 and only three defending it. The two ways of bringing a fourth one to the defense spell Black's doom.

25. . . .   KR—B2

If 25. . . . R—Kt1, defending his first rank, White would play 26. R—Kt4!, with the threat 27. QxRP ch, KxQ; 28. R—R4 mate (mate No. 17A).

26. BxKt   resigns.

Black loses a Piece without any compensation, and the attack remains strong. Let us emphasize the subtlety of White's twenty-second move, which meets an eventual counterattack on the Queen by a latent threat of mate in three. This shows how in many games the possible moves and combinations are more interesting than the moves which are actually played. The role of the commentator is to show them to the reader.

CHAPTER 26: *Solution to Quizzes*

−1−

1. R−R5 ch   K−Kt2
2. RxKtP dis mate.

−2−

1. . . .   RxP ch
2. KxR or RxR   QxRP mate.

−3−

1. RxB ch   KxR or K−Kt1
2. Q−Kt7 mate.

−4−

1. B−B6 ch   KtxB
2. PxKt mate.

−5−

1. RxB ch   KxR
2. Q−B7 mate.

−6−

1. Q−B5 ch   KtxQ
2. P−K6 mate.

This position is taken from the Muzio Gambit.

−7−

1. Kt−B6 double ch   K−B1
2. Q−K8 mate.

An elementary example of the double check.

−8−

1. Q−R7 ch !   KxQ
2. R−K7 double ch   K−R1
3. R−R7 mate.

−9−

1. Kt−Kt5 dis ch   K−K1
2. Kt−Q6 mate.

−10−

1. Q−K8 ch !   KxQ
2. Kt−B6 ch !   K−Q1
3. Kt−B7 mate.

−11−

1. . . .   Kt−Q5 ch
2. KxR   Kt−K6 ch
3. K−B1   Kt−K7 mate.

−12−

1. . . .   QxR ch
2. KxQ   Kt−K7 ch
3. K−R1   Kt−B7 mate.

−13−

1. . . .   QxP ch !

To place the King in a position where it will be double checked and also to obtain control of White's KKt3.

2. KxQ   R−R4 double ch
3. K−Kt1   B−R7 ch
4. K−R1   Kt−Kt6 mate.

— 14 —

1. Q—R7 ch	K—B1
2. Q—R8 ch	K—K2
3. Kt—B5 ch !	PxKt
4. B—B5 double ch and mate.	

— 15 —

1. R—K8 ch	B—Q1
2. RxB ch	RxR
3. Kt—B7 ch	K—Kt1
4. Kt—R6 double ch	K—R1
5. Q—Kt8 ch	RxQ
6. Kt—B7 mate.	

— 16 —

1. Q—K5 ch	K—R1
2. Kt—B7 ch	K—Kt1
3. KtxR ch	K—R1
4. Kt—B7 ch, etc.	

Now that the pinning Rook has disappeared, the same as above.

— 17 —

1. Kt—Kt6 ch	PxKt
2. Q—R3 mate.	

This is Greco's mate No. 3, with the difference that Black's Kt1 is obstructed instead of being guarded.

— 18 —

29. . . .	BxP ch
30. RxB	Q—K8 ch
31. R—Kt1	Q or RxR mate.

Or else:

30. K—Kt1	B—Q5 dis ch
31. R—Kt2	Q—K8 ch

If 31. K—B2, Q—Kt8 mate.

32. K—B2	RxR mate.

— 19 —

1. Q—B5 ch	PxQ
2. R—Q8 mate.	

This is a form of Anastasia's mate in the middle of the board.

— 20 —

1. . . .	Kt—Kt6 ch
2. RxKt	RxKt ch
3. KxR	R—R8 mate.

Anastasia's mate.

— 21 —

1. . . .	QxP ch
2. PxQ	B—R6 mate.

— 22 —

1. . . .	QxP ch
2. PxQ	B—R6 mate.

(21 and 22 are twin problems)

— 23 —

1. QxP ch	PxQ
2. B—Q4 ch	B—K4
3. BxB ch	R—B3
4. BxR mate.	

(Mate No. 7B)

— 24 —

1. . . .	Q—R4
2. B—K2	

Or else . . . Q—R6, followed by mate.

3. . . .   Kt—Kt5
4. P—KR4   QxRP
5. PxQ   B—R7 mate.

(Blackburne's mate)

—25—

1. Kt—Kt6 ch   K—Ktl

If 1. . . . BPxKt; 2. RxP
ch, KxR; 3. R—R1 mate,
yielding the typical position
of mate No. 2. Now, however,
White will be able to place
Anastasia's mate.

2. Kt—K7 ch   K—R1
3. RxP ch   KxR
4. R—R1 mate.

—26—

1. QR—B1 !   QxQ?

It was necessary to play 1.
. . . QxR ch. Now there is
mate in four moves.

2. Kt—Kt6 ch   K—Ktl
3. Kt—K7 ch   K—R1
4. RxP ch   KxR
5. R—R1 mate.

—27—

1. Q—Kt6 !

Threatening mate. If 1.
. . . RPxQ; 2. Kt—K7 mate.
If 1. . . . BPxQ; 2. Kt—K7
ch, K—R1; 3. RxR mate. If 1.
. . . P—KR3; 2. RxRP, etc.
And if 1. . . . Q—K5; 2. Kt—
K7 ch, and mate next move.

1. . . .   QxQ
2. Kt—K7 ch   K—R1
3. KtxQ ch   K—Ktl
4. Kt—K7 ch   K—R1
5. RxP ch   KxR
6. R—R3 ch   R—R5
7. RxR mate.

—28—

1. . . .   R—R1 ch
2. RxR   Q—Kt4 ch
3. K—Ktl   Kt—Q7 ch
4. K—B1   Kt—Kt6
                double ch
5. K—Ktl   Q—B8 ch
6. RxQ   Kt—Q7 ch
7. K—R2   R—R1 ch
8. Q interposes RxQ mate.

This mate partakes both of
Lucena's and Anastasia's
mates.

—29—

There is an obvious mate:

31. RxP ch   KxR

If 31. . . . K—Ktl; 32. R
xP ch, and mate next move.

32. Q—R5 ch   K—Ktl
33. Q—B7 ch   K—R2
34. QxP mate.

—30—

In order to mate the Black
King it is necessary to deprive
it of its flight square, B2, by
advancing the Kt's Pawn. But
1. P—Kt6 would be met by 1.

. . . QxP. How did Alekhine solve the problem?

1. Kt—K5 !   PxKt

The only move. If 1. . . . QxKt; 2. P—Kt6, and mate next move, and if 1. . . . P—KKt3; 2. R—R8 ch !, followed by mate.

2. P—Kt6   QxP
3. Q—B4 ch   B—Q4
4. QxB ch   Q or R—B2
5. R—R8 mate.

—31—

The Knight prevents mate on White's Kt2. Moreover, if 1. PxP, BPxP, and the RP is covered by the Queen. A Queen sacrifice however will enable Black to mate (No. 9).

1. . . .   QxRP ch
2. KxQ   PxP double ch
3. K—Kt1   R—R8 mate.

—32—

1. . . .   B—K5 dis ch
2. Kt—Kt2   RxKt ch
3. K—R1   R—Kt8
              double ch
4. KxR   R—Kt1 ch
5. B—R4   RxB mate.

—33—

1. QxP ch   RxQ
2. R—K8 ch   R—B1
3. RxR ch   KxR
4. R—K8 mate (mate No. 1
   and No. 9).

—34—

White is threatening with Lolli's mate No. 9.

31. RxP ch   PxR
32. QxP ch   K—Kt1
33. Q—R8 mate.

30. . . . Q—B4 is not sufficient on account of 31. Kt—K7. But Black can play 30. . . . BxP!!, threatening the corridor mate. 31. RxP ch?, B—R3!, etc.

—35—

1. BxKt   P—Kt3

If . . . PxB; 2. QxP ch, followed by mate; and if . . . P—B3; 2. B—B1 dis ch, QxQ; 3. RxQ mate.

2. QxP ch !   PxQ
3. BxR mate.

—36—

Because of the following answer:

27. QxP ch !! KtxQ
28. R—Q8 ch   Kt—B1
29. R—R8 ch   KxR
30. RxKt mate.

—37—

1. . . .   B—Kt8 ch
2. K—R1   R—Kt6
3. QxR   QxQ
4. R—B2   QxR
5. ad lib.   Q—R7 mate.

-38-

In this position, White played 1. Q–Kt4?, and after ... BxKt, 2. QxB drew in the end-game. Henneberger could have mated in five:

1. B–Kt7 ch !   RxB
2. R–B8 ch   R–Kt1
3. Q–Kt4 !

Threatening simultaneously 4. QxR mate, 4. Q–Kt7 mate and also 4. RxR mate.

3. . . .   Q–Q1
4. RxQ

And mate follows next move, for Black cannot meet the three threats at the same time.

-39-

This mate, which is reminiscent of a position composed by Stamma, is one of the most extraordinary to which a Grand Master has ever been subjected.

1. . . .   Kt–K7 ch !
2. RxKt   R–B8 ch !
3. KxR   Q–R8 ch
4. K–B2   Kt–Kt5 mate.

-40-

17. PxP ch   KxP
18. QxKt ch   KxQ
19. Kt–K6 dis ch K–R4

20. R–B5 ch   K–R5
21. R–B4 ch   K–R4
22. Kt–Kt7 ch

(a)

22. . . .   K–Kt4
23. P–R4 ch   K–R3
24. RxP dis ch   B–K6
25. BxB mate.

(b)

22. . . .   K–R3
23. RxP dis ch   B–K6
24. BxB mate.

-41-

The solution of this exercise is not easy to find, although it is a typical mate.

1. B–K7 ch   K–K1
2. B–B6 dis ch   K–B1
3. Q–K7 ch   K–Kt1
4. QxB mate.

-42-

1. . . .   Q–R8 ch
2. KxQ   B–B6 ch
3. K–Kt1   RxR ch
4. BxR   RxB mate.

-43-

1. B–R6 ch   K–Kt1
2. Q–Kt5 ch !   QxQ
3. R–K8 ch   B–B1
4. RxB mate.

-44-

1. R–K8 ch   Kt–B1
2. Kt–R6 ch   QxKt
3. RxKt ch   KxR
4. Q–Q8 mate.

This is mate No. 15.

—45—

1. Kt—B6 ch !

To force the opening of the Kt's file.

1. . . .	PxKt
2. Q—B8 ch !	KxQ
3. B—R6 ch	K—Kt1
4. R—K8 mate.	

Bringing about mate No. 14C.

—46—

1. Q—Q5 ch !

Black cannot take the Queen on account of R—K8 mate.

1. . . .	K—B1
2. Q—Q7 ch	K—Kt1
3. Q—Q8 ch	Kt—B1
4. QxKt ch	KxQ
5. R—K8 mate.	

Mate No. 15B.

—47—

1. Q—Q7 ch	BxQ
2. Kt—Q6 double ch	K—Q1
3. Kt—B7 ch	K—B1
4. R—K8 ch	BxR
5. R—Q8 mate.	

Mate No. 15B.

—48—

| 1. QxB ! | RxR |

The best move. If 1. . . . QxB; 2. RxQ, RxR ch; 3. K—Kt2 and wins. If 1. . . . Px

Q?; 2. B—K5 dis ch !; Q—Kt5; 3. RxQ ch, K—R1; 4. BxP mate (Morphy's mate No. 14).

2. QxKtP ch !	KxQ
3. B—K5 double ch	K—R3
4. B—Kt7 ch	K—R4
5. B—K2 ch	

And Black has the choice between:

| 5. . . . | K—R5 |
| 6. B—B6 mate. | |

Or:

5. . . .	Q—Kt5
6. BxQ ch	K—Kt4
7. BxR ch	King plays
8. BxR and wins.	

The Morphy mate threat has brought about a winning end-game.

—49—

In this position Black played:

| 32. . . . | Q—Kt3 ! |

And White resigned. The threat is 33. . . . QxR ch; 34. KxQ, R—B8 ch; 35. Q covers, RxQ mate (mate No. 14C).

Are there any means of meeting the threat? Let us first try capturing the Queen.

33. RxQ	R—B8 ch
34. R—Kt1	RxR ch
35. KxR	R—B8 ch
36. Q covers	RxQ mate.

Again mate No. 14C. Let us now try to give a double protection to the first rank.

33. R—R1   R—B8 !

Threatening a form of pinned mate 34. ... Q—Kt7 mate. 34. QRxR is not sufficient on account of 34. ... RxR, and White will have to play 35. Q—K1, RxQ, and mate next move.

34. Q—K1 !	QxR ch
35. KxQ	RxQ ch
36. RxR	R—Kt1 and wins

—50—

1. QxKt ch	RxQ
2. PxP ch	K—K2
3. B—B5 mate.	

—51—

1. R—B8 !	RxR
2. RxR	BxR
3. QxQ mate.	

Or else:

| 2. ... | QxR |
| 3. Q—K7 mate. | |

—52—

1. RxKt	QxR
2. Q—B6 ch !	PxQ
3. BxP mate.	

Typical aspect of the Boden mate.

—53—

| 1. QxP ch ! | PxQ |

If 1. ... Kt—R3; 2. QxKt ch, K—Kt1; 3. QxB mate.

2. P—Kt6 ch	KxP
3. R—Kt1 ch	K—R2
4. RxB mate.	

After an introductory maneuver, Damiano's mate No. 17 was brought about.

—54—

| 1. R—R7 ch | KxR |

If ... K—Kt1 or B1, then 2. QxP mate; and if ... K—Kt3; 2. Q—B5 mate, or QxP mate.

2. QxP ch	K—R1
3. R—R1 ch	R—R3
4. RxR mate.	

—55—

1. Q—Kt8 ch !	KxQ
2. R—K8 ch	RxR
3. RxR mate.	

—56—

| 1. Q—Kt5 ch | PxQ |
| 2. BxP mate. | |

—57—

1. RxB	QxR
2. RxKt	PxR
3. Kt—B5	Q—K5

If 3. ... Q—K3; 4. Q—B4, K—R1; 5. Q—R6.

| 4. Q—Kt5 ch ! | PxQ |
| 5. Kt—R6 mate. | |

Mate No. 19B. There are several other ways of winning but not so direct.

—58—

1. QxKt!   PxQ

If 1. . . . castles; 2. QxKtP ch, KxQ; 3. B—B6 ch, K—Kt1; 4. Kt—R6 mate (mate No. 19B).

2. KtxP ch   K—B1
3. B—R6 mate.

And this is mate No. 19A.

—59—

1. RxP ch

Black has the choice between:

1. . . .   RPxR
2. Q—R8 mate.

Or else:

1. . . .   BPxR
2. Kt—K7 (double check) mate.

In the first case we have mate No. 9 and in the second case mate No. 20.

—60—

1. RxP ch   KtxR

If 1. . . . K—R1; 2. RxP ch, KxR; 3. Q—R3 ch, K—Kt1; 4. R—Kt1 ch, Kt covers; 5. RxKt mate (Damiano's mate No. 17).

2. Kt—R6 ch   K—R1
3. KtxP ch   RxKt
4. KtxR ch   K—Kt1
5. Kt—R6 double ch   K—R1
6. Q—Kt8 ch   RxQ
7. Kt—B7 mate.

Lucena's mate is brought about by a neat sacrifice.

—61—

1. QxR ch   KxQ
2. Kt—Q4 dis ch   K—B1

If 2. . . . Q—K4; 3. R—Kt8 ch, K—K2; 4. Kt—B5 mate.

3. R—K8 ch !

The preparatory sacrifice for mate No. 18.

3. . . .   KxR
4. R—Kt8 ch   K—K2
5. Kt—B5 mate.

—62—

1. . . .   RxP

Threatening mate No. 9.

2. KxR

If 2. QxQ, KtxQ mate (Arabian mate).

2. . . .   R—R1 ch
3. K—Kt1   QxKt ch
4. PxQ   Kt—B6 double ch
5. K—Kt2   R—R7 mate.

—63—

1. RxP ch   PxR
2. Kt—B6 ch   K—R1

3. R—Kt7 !   KxR
4. Kt—K8 double ch K—Kt3
5. Q—B6 ch   K—R4
6. Kt—Kt7 mate.

–64–

1. . . .   Kt—Kt6 ch
2. K—Kt1   QxP ch
3. RxQ   KtxP mate.

–65–

1. Kt—Kt6 ch   K—Kt1
2. Q—Kt7 ch   RxQ
3. Kt—R6 mate.

Both mates are mate No. 21.

–66–

1. . . .   Kt—B6
2. resigns.

The threat of the Arabian mate (2. . . . QxP) forces the answer:

2. PxKt   R—Q7

Mate is inevitable, as White cannot cover his second rank.

–67–

1. QxB ch   K—Q5
2. B—K3 ch   KxB
3. Q—B2 mate.

The King is drawn into a mating net.

–68–

1. Q—B8 ch   K—Q2
2. B—K6 ch !   KxB
3. Q—B5 mate.

The same stratagem as in the preceding example.

–69–

This position occurred in the last round of the Carlsbad Tournament, 1907. Rubinstein needed only half a point to win first prize. For this reason he played 24. . . . B—R3?, bringing about a rapid exchange of Pieces and drawing the game. He had overlooked a mate or a forced win, thus:

24. . . .   R—KR4 !
25. P—KR3   Kt—Kt5 ! !
26. PxKt   RxP ch
27. K—Kt1   Q—R7 ch
28. K—B1   Q—R8 ch
29. K—K2   QxP mate.

Or else:

25. P—Kt3   QxP
26. B—K4   RxR
27. RxR   KtxB
28. PxKt   BxP ch
29. QxB   QxP mate.

–70–

1. . . .   QxR ch
2. KxQ   RxP ch
3. K—Kt1   R—B8 ch
4. K—Kt2   R(1)—B7 mate.

If 3. K—K1, R—K7 ch; 4. K—Q1, R—B8 mate.

–71–

1. QxP ch   K—R1

If 1. . . . KxQ; 2. R—Kt3 mate.

| 2. BxKt | PxB |

If 2. . . . RxKt; 3. Q—R7 mate; and if . . . Q—B2; 3. QxP ch, R—R2; 4. QxR mate.

| 3. QxP ch | R—R2 |
| 4. QxR(B1) mate. | |

This is the Arabian mate.

—72—

1. QxB . . . (if 1. . . . QxQ)	
2. Kt—Q7 ch	K—R1
3. Kt—B6 dis ch	Kt—R3
4. Kt—Kt6 mate.	

—73—

1. Q—K8 ch	B—Q1
2. QxP ch !	KxQ
3. B—Kt4 ch	K—Q3
4. R—K6 ch	K—Q2
5. R—K5 dis ch	K—Q3
6. P—B5 mate.	

—74—

1. . . .	R—R4 ch
2. KxR	Q—R6 ch
3. K—Kt4	P—R3 ch
4. K—B4	P—Kt4 ch
5. K—K5	Q—K3 mate.

—75—

In this game, Hromadka, in time trouble, played 35. . . . Q—Kt7 ch, ruining his winning position and losing the game. Had he not been so sorely pressed by time he could either:

(a) Have won the Queen:

| 35. . . . | B—B4 ? ! |

And the Queen is lost, because, if it goes to its Q5, mate follows very soon:

36. Q—Q5	Q—Kt7 ch
37. K—K1	Q—B7 ch !
38. BxQ	PxB ch
39. K—B1	Kt—K6 mate.

(b) Or mated in a definite number of moves:

| 35. . . . | R—B7 ch |
| 36. BxR | |

If 36. K—K1, QxKt ch; 37. B—B1, QxB mate.

36. . . .	B—R6 ch
37. K—K1	PxB ch
38. KxP	Q—Kt7 ch
39. K—K1	Q—Kt6 mate.

—76—

1. Q—R4 ch	KxP
2. Q—R5 ch	K—B3
3. B—Kt5 ch	K—K4
4. B—K7 !	P—QB5
5. R—K1 ch	Q—K6 ch
6. RxQ mate.	

—77—

1. Q—R7 ch	KxQ
2. RxP ch	RxR
3. Kt—B6 ch	K—Kt3
4. B—R5 ch	K—B4
5. P—Kt4 ch	RxP
6. PxR mate.	

—78—

1. Kt—R6 ch   K—R1
2. KtxR ch   K—Kt1
3. RxP mate.

—79—

1. B—Q8 ch   K—R2
2. RxP ch   PxR

If 2. . . . KxR?; 3. Q—R5 mate; and if 2. . . . K—Kt1; 3. Q—B4 ch, followed by mate in three.

    3. Q—Q7 ch   K—Kt1 !
    4. Q—B7 ch   K—R1
    5. Q—B8 ch   K—R2
    6. B—Kt6 ch KxB
    7. Q—Kt8 mate.

A typical form of the "Ép- aulettes" mate. Although this position was composed, it is quite plausible and likely to be met in practice.

—80—

1. . . .   Q—K8 ch
2. B—Kt1   Kt—B7 ch
3. K—Kt2   Q—K5 ch
4. K—B1   Q—Q6 ch
5. K—Kt2   Q—B6 ch
6. K—B1   Kt—K5 dis ch
7. K—K1   Q—B8 mate.

The clever problem composer, Edward Pape, has demonstrated in this exercise that the qualities required for composing problems also find their application in games.

A CATALOG OF SELECTED
DOVER BOOKS
IN ALL FIELDS OF INTEREST

A CATALOG OF SELECTED DOVER BOOKS IN ALL FIELDS OF INTEREST

100 BEST-LOVED POEMS, Edited by Philip Smith. "The Passionate Shepherd to His Love," "Shall I compare thee to a summer's day?" "Death, be not proud," "The Raven," "The Road Not Taken," plus works by Blake, Wordsworth, Byron, Shelley, Keats, many others. 96pp. 5$\frac{3}{16}$ x 8$\frac{1}{4}$. 0-486-28553-7

100 SMALL HOUSES OF THE THIRTIES, Brown-Blodgett Company. Exterior photographs and floor plans for 100 charming structures. Illustrations of models accompanied by descriptions of interiors, color schemes, closet space, and other amenities. 200 illustrations. 112pp. 8$\frac{3}{8}$ x 11. 0-486-44131-8

1000 TURN-OF-THE-CENTURY HOUSES: With Illustrations and Floor Plans, Herbert C. Chivers. Reproduced from a rare edition, this showcase of homes ranges from cottages and bungalows to sprawling mansions. Each house is meticulously illustrated and accompanied by complete floor plans. 256pp. 9$\frac{3}{8}$ x 12$\frac{1}{4}$. 0-486-45596-3

101 GREAT AMERICAN POEMS, Edited by The American Poetry & Literacy Project. Rich treasury of verse from the 19th and 20th centuries includes works by Edgar Allan Poe, Robert Frost, Walt Whitman, Langston Hughes, Emily Dickinson, T. S. Eliot, other notables. 96pp. 5$\frac{3}{16}$ x 8$\frac{1}{4}$. 0-486-40158-8

101 GREAT SAMURAI PRINTS, Utagawa Kuniyoshi. Kuniyoshi was a master of the warrior woodblock print — and these 18th-century illustrations represent the pinnacle of his craft. Full-color portraits of renowned Japanese samurais pulse with movement, passion, and remarkably fine detail. 112pp. 8$\frac{3}{8}$ x 11. 0-486-46523-3

ABC OF BALLET, Janet Grosser. Clearly worded, abundantly illustrated little guide defines basic ballet-related terms: arabesque, battement, pas de chat, relevé, sissonne, many others. Pronunciation guide included. Excellent primer. 48pp. 4$\frac{3}{16}$ x 5$\frac{3}{4}$. 0-486-40871-X

ACCESSORIES OF DRESS: An Illustrated Encyclopedia, Katherine Lester and Bess Viola Oerke. Illustrations of hats, veils, wigs, cravats, shawls, shoes, gloves, and other accessories enhance an engaging commentary that reveals the humor and charm of the many-sided story of accessorized apparel. 644 figures and 59 plates. 608pp. 6 $\frac{1}{8}$ x 9$\frac{1}{4}$. 0-486-43378-1

ADVENTURES OF HUCKLEBERRY FINN, Mark Twain. Join Huck and Jim as their boyhood adventures along the Mississippi River lead them into a world of excitement, danger, and self-discovery. Humorous narrative, lyrical descriptions of the Mississippi valley, and memorable characters. 224pp. 5$\frac{3}{16}$ x 8$\frac{1}{4}$. 0-486-28061-6

ALICE STARMORE'S BOOK OF FAIR ISLE KNITTING, Alice Starmore. A noted designer from the region of Scotland's Fair Isle explores the history and techniques of this distinctive, stranded-color knitting style and provides copious illustrated instructions for 14 original knitwear designs. 208pp. 8$\frac{3}{8}$ x 10$\frac{7}{8}$. 0-486-47218-3

CATALOG OF DOVER BOOKS

ALICE'S ADVENTURES IN WONDERLAND, Lewis Carroll. Beloved classic about a little girl lost in a topsy-turvy land and her encounters with the White Rabbit, March Hare, Mad Hatter, Cheshire Cat, and other delightfully improbable characters. 42 illustrations by Sir John Tenniel. 96pp. 5³⁄₁₆ x 8¼.   0-486-27543-4

AMERICA'S LIGHTHOUSES: An Illustrated History, Francis Ross Holland. Profusely illustrated fact-filled survey of American lighthouses since 1716. Over 200 stations — East, Gulf, and West coasts, Great Lakes, Hawaii, Alaska, Puerto Rico, the Virgin Islands, and the Mississippi and St. Lawrence Rivers. 240pp. 8 x 10¾.
0-486-25576-X

AN ENCYCLOPEDIA OF THE VIOLIN, Alberto Bachmann. Translated by Frederick H. Martens. Introduction by Eugene Ysaye. First published in 1925, this renowned reference remains unsurpassed as a source of essential information, from construction and evolution to repertoire and technique. Includes a glossary and 73 illustrations. 496pp. 6⅛ x 9¼.   0-486-46618-3

ANIMALS: 1,419 Copyright-Free Illustrations of Mammals, Birds, Fish, Insects, etc., Selected by Jim Harter. Selected for its visual impact and ease of use, this outstanding collection of wood engravings presents over 1,000 species of animals in extremely lifelike poses. Includes mammals, birds, reptiles, amphibians, fish, insects, and other invertebrates. 284pp. 9 x 12.   0-486-23766-4

THE ANNALS, Tacitus. Translated by Alfred John Church and William Jackson Brodribb. This vital chronicle of Imperial Rome, written by the era's great historian, spans A.D. 14-68 and paints incisive psychological portraits of major figures, from Tiberius to Nero. 416pp. 5³⁄₁₆ x 8¼.   0-486-45236-0

ANTIGONE, Sophocles. Filled with passionate speeches and sensitive probing of moral and philosophical issues, this powerful and often-performed Greek drama reveals the grim fate that befalls the children of Oedipus. Footnotes. 64pp. 5³⁄₁₆ x 8 ¼.   0-486-27804-2

ART DECO DECORATIVE PATTERNS IN FULL COLOR, Christian Stoll. Reprinted from a rare 1910 portfolio, 160 sensuous and exotic images depict a breathtaking array of florals, geometrics, and abstracts — all elegant in their stark simplicity. 64pp. 8⅜ x 11.   0-486-44862-2

THE ARTHUR RACKHAM TREASURY: 86 Full-Color Illustrations, Arthur Rackham. Selected and Edited by Jeff A. Menges. A stunning treasury of 86 full-page plates span the famed English artist's career, from *Rip Van Winkle* (1905) to masterworks such as *Undine*, *A Midsummer Night's Dream*, and *Wind in the Willows* (1939). 96pp. 8⅜ x 11.
0-486-44685-9

THE AUTHENTIC GILBERT & SULLIVAN SONGBOOK, W. S. Gilbert and A. S. Sullivan. The most comprehensive collection available, this songbook includes selections from every one of Gilbert and Sullivan's light operas. Ninety-two numbers are presented uncut and unedited, and in their original keys. 410pp. 9 x 12.
0-486-23482-7

THE AWAKENING, Kate Chopin. First published in 1899, this controversial novel of a New Orleans wife's search for love outside a stifling marriage shocked readers. Today, it remains a first-rate narrative with superb characterization. New introductory Note. 128pp. 5³⁄₁₆ x 8¼.   0-486-27786-0

BASIC DRAWING, Louis Priscilla. Beginning with perspective, this commonsense manual progresses to the figure in movement, light and shade, anatomy, drapery, composition, trees and landscape, and outdoor sketching. Black-and-white illustrations throughout. 128pp. 8⅜ x 11.   0-486-45815-6

Browse over 9,000 books at www.doverpublications.com

CATALOG OF DOVER BOOKS

THE BATTLES THAT CHANGED HISTORY, Fletcher Pratt. Historian profiles 16 crucial conflicts, ancient to modern, that changed the course of Western civilization. Gripping accounts of battles led by Alexander the Great, Joan of Arc, Ulysses S. Grant, other commanders. 27 maps. 352pp. 5⅜ x 8½. 0-486-41129-X

BEETHOVEN'S LETTERS, Ludwig van Beethoven. Edited by Dr. A. C. Kalischer. Features 457 letters to fellow musicians, friends, greats, patrons, and literary men. Reveals musical thoughts, quirks of personality, insights, and daily events. Includes 15 plates. 410pp. 5⅜ x 8½. 0-486-22769-3

BERNICE BOBS HER HAIR AND OTHER STORIES, F. Scott Fitzgerald. This brilliant anthology includes 6 of Fitzgerald's most popular stories: "The Diamond as Big as the Ritz," the title tale, "The Offshore Pirate," "The Ice Palace," "The Jelly Bean," and "May Day." 176pp. 5⅜ x 8½. 0-486-47049-0

BESLER'S BOOK OF FLOWERS AND PLANTS: 73 Full-Color Plates from Hortus Eystettensis, 1613, Basilius Besler. Here is a selection of magnificent plates from the Hortus Eystettensis, which vividly illustrated and identified the plants, flowers, and trees that thrived in the legendary German garden at Eichstätt. 80pp. 8⅜ x 11. 0-486-46005-3

THE BOOK OF KELLS, Edited by Blanche Cirker. Painstakingly reproduced from a rare facsimile edition, this volume contains full-page decorations, portraits, illustrations, plus a sampling of textual leaves with exquisite calligraphy and ornamentation. 32 full-color illustrations. 32pp. 9⅜ x 12¼. 0-486-24345-1

THE BOOK OF THE CROSSBOW: With an Additional Section on Catapults and Other Siege Engines, Ralph Payne-Gallwey. Fascinating study traces history and use of crossbow as military and sporting weapon, from Middle Ages to modern times. Also covers related weapons: balistas, catapults, Turkish bows, more. Over 240 illustrations. 400pp. 7¼ x 10⅛. 0-486-28720-3

THE BUNGALOW BOOK: Floor Plans and Photos of 112 Houses, 1910, Henry L. Wilson. Here are 112 of the most popular and economic blueprints of the early 20th century — plus an illustration or photograph of each completed house. A wonderful time capsule that still offers a wealth of valuable insights. 160pp. 8⅜ x 11. 0-486-45104-6

THE CALL OF THE WILD, Jack London. A classic novel of adventure, drawn from London's own experiences as a Klondike adventurer, relating the story of a heroic dog caught in the brutal life of the Alaska Gold Rush. Note. 64pp. 5³⁄₁₆ x 8¼. 0-486-26472-6

CANDIDE, Voltaire. Edited by Francois-Marie Arouet. One of the world's great satires since its first publication in 1759. Witty, caustic skewering of romance, science, philosophy, religion, government — nearly all human ideals and institutions. 112pp. 5³⁄₁₆ x 8¼. 0-486-26689-3

CELEBRATED IN THEIR TIME: Photographic Portraits from the George Grantham Bain Collection, Edited by Amy Pastan. With an Introduction by Michael Carlebach. Remarkable portrait gallery features 112 rare images of Albert Einstein, Charlie Chaplin, the Wright Brothers, Henry Ford, and other luminaries from the worlds of politics, art, entertainment, and industry. 128pp. 8⅜ x 11. 0-486-46754-6

CHARIOTS FOR APOLLO: The NASA History of Manned Lunar Spacecraft to 1969, Courtney G. Brooks, James M. Grimwood, and Loyd S. Swenson, Jr. This illustrated history by a trio of experts is the definitive reference on the Apollo spacecraft and lunar modules. It traces the vehicles' design, development, and operation in space. More than 100 photographs and illustrations. 576pp. 6¾ x 9¼. 0-486-46756-2

Browse over 9,000 books at www.doverpublications.com

A CHRISTMAS CAROL, Charles Dickens. This engrossing tale relates Ebenezer Scrooge's ghostly journeys through Christmases past, present, and future and his ultimate transformation from a harsh and grasping old miser to a charitable and compassionate human being. 80pp. 5³⁄₁₆ x 8¼. 0-486-26865-9

COMMON SENSE, Thomas Paine. First published in January of 1776, this highly influential landmark document clearly and persuasively argued for American separation from Great Britain and paved the way for the Declaration of Independence. 64pp. 5³⁄₁₆ x 8¼. 0-486-29602-4

THE COMPLETE SHORT STORIES OF OSCAR WILDE, Oscar Wilde. Complete texts of "The Happy Prince and Other Tales," "A House of Pomegranates," "Lord Arthur Savile's Crime and Other Stories," "Poems in Prose," and "The Portrait of Mr. W. H." 208pp. 5³⁄₁₆ x 8¼. 0-486-45216-6

COMPLETE SONNETS, William Shakespeare. Over 150 exquisite poems deal with love, friendship, the tyranny of time, beauty's evanescence, death, and other themes in language of remarkable power, precision, and beauty. Glossary of archaic terms. 80pp. 5³⁄₁₆ x 8¼. 0-486-26686-9

THE COUNT OF MONTE CRISTO: Abridged Edition, Alexandre Dumas. Falsely accused of treason, Edmond Dantès is imprisoned in the bleak Chateau d'If. After a hair-raising escape, he launches an elaborate plot to extract a bitter revenge against those who betrayed him. 448pp. 5³⁄₁₆ x 8¼. 0-486-45643-9

CRAFTSMAN BUNGALOWS: Designs from the Pacific Northwest, Yoho & Merritt. This reprint of a rare catalog, showcasing the charming simplicity and cozy style of Craftsman bungalows, is filled with photos of completed homes, plus floor plans and estimated costs. An indispensable resource for architects, historians, and illustrators. 112pp. 10 x 7. 0-486-46875-5

CRAFTSMAN BUNGALOWS: 59 Homes from "The Craftsman," Edited by Gustav Stickley. Best and most attractive designs from Arts and Crafts Movement publication — 1903–1916 — includes sketches, photographs of homes, floor plans, descriptive text. 128pp. 8¼ x 11. 0-486-25829-7

CRIME AND PUNISHMENT, Fyodor Dostoyevsky. Translated by Constance Garnett. Supreme masterpiece tells the story of Raskolnikov, a student tormented by his own thoughts after he murders an old woman. Overwhelmed by guilt and terror, he confesses and goes to prison. 480pp. 5³⁄₁₆ x 8¼. 0-486-41587-2

THE DECLARATION OF INDEPENDENCE AND OTHER GREAT DOCUMENTS OF AMERICAN HISTORY: 1775-1865, Edited by John Grafton. Thirteen compelling and influential documents: Henry's "Give Me Liberty or Give Me Death," Declaration of Independence, The Constitution, Washington's First Inaugural Address, The Monroe Doctrine, The Emancipation Proclamation, Gettysburg Address, more. 64pp. 5³⁄₁₆ x 8¼. 0-486-41124-9

THE DESERT AND THE SOWN: Travels in Palestine and Syria, Gertrude Bell. "The female Lawrence of Arabia," Gertrude Bell wrote captivating, perceptive accounts of her travels in the Middle East. This intriguing narrative, accompanied by 160 photos, traces her 1905 sojourn in Lebanon, Syria, and Palestine. 368pp. 5⅜ x 8½. 0-486-46876-3

A DOLL'S HOUSE, Henrik Ibsen. Ibsen's best-known play displays his genius for realistic prose drama. An expression of women's rights, the play climaxes when the central character, Nora, rejects a smothering marriage and life in "a doll's house." 80pp. 5³⁄₁₆ x 8¼. 0-486-27062-9

Browse over 9,000 books at www.doverpublications.com

DOOMED SHIPS: Great Ocean Liner Disasters, William H. Miller, Jr. Nearly 200 photographs, many from private collections, highlight tales of some of the vessels whose pleasure cruises ended in catastrophe: the *Morro Castle, Normandie, Andrea Doria, Europa,* and many others. 128pp. 8⅞ x 11¼. 0-486-45366-9

THE DORÉ BIBLE ILLUSTRATIONS, Gustave Doré. Detailed plates from the Bible: the Creation scenes, Adam and Eve, horrifying visions of the Flood, the battle sequences with their monumental crowds, depictions of the life of Jesus, 241 plates in all. 241pp. 9 x 12. 0-486-23004-X

DRAWING DRAPERY FROM HEAD TO TOE, Cliff Young. Expert guidance on how to draw shirts, pants, skirts, gloves, hats, and coats on the human figure, including folds in relation to the body, pull and crush, action folds, creases, more. Over 200 drawings. 48pp. 8¼ x 11. 0-486-45591-2

DUBLINERS, James Joyce. A fine and accessible introduction to the work of one of the 20th century's most influential writers, this collection features 15 tales, including a masterpiece of the short-story genre, "The Dead." 160pp. 5³⁄₁₆ x 8¼. 0-486-26870-5

EASY-TO-MAKE POP-UPS, Joan Irvine. Illustrated by Barbara Reid. Dozens of wonderful ideas for three-dimensional paper fun — from holiday greeting cards with moving parts to a pop-up menagerie. Easy-to-follow, illustrated instructions for more than 30 projects. 299 black-and-white illustrations. 96pp. 8⅜ x 11. 0-486-44622-0

EASY-TO-MAKE STORYBOOK DOLLS: A "Novel" Approach to Cloth Dollmaking, Sherralyn St. Clair. Favorite fictional characters come alive in this unique beginner's dollmaking guide. Includes patterns for Pollyanna, Dorothy from *The Wonderful Wizard of Oz*, Mary of *The Secret Garden*, plus easy-to-follow instructions, 263 black-and-white illustrations, and an 8-page color insert. 112pp. 8¼ x 11. 0-486-47360-0

EINSTEIN'S ESSAYS IN SCIENCE, Albert Einstein. Speeches and essays in accessible, everyday language profile influential physicists such as Niels Bohr and Isaac Newton. They also explore areas of physics to which the author made major contributions. 128pp. 5 x 8. 0-486-47011-3

EL DORADO: Further Adventures of the Scarlet Pimpernel, Baroness Orczy. A popular sequel to *The Scarlet Pimpernel,* this suspenseful story recounts the Pimpernel's attempts to rescue the Dauphin from imprisonment during the French Revolution. An irresistible blend of intrigue, period detail, and vibrant characterizations. 352pp. 5³⁄₁₆ x 8¼. 0-486-44026-5

ELEGANT SMALL HOMES OF THE TWENTIES: 99 Designs from a Competition, Chicago Tribune. Nearly 100 designs for five- and six-room houses feature New England and Southern colonials, Normandy cottages, stately Italianate dwellings, and other fascinating snapshots of American domestic architecture of the 1920s. 112pp. 9 x 12. 0-486-46910-7

THE ELEMENTS OF STYLE: The Original Edition, William Strunk, Jr. This is the book that generations of writers have relied upon for timeless advice on grammar, diction, syntax, and other essentials. In concise terms, it identifies the principal requirements of proper style and common errors. 64pp. 5⅜ x 8½. 0-486-44798-7

THE ELUSIVE PIMPERNEL, Baroness Orczy. Robespierre's revolutionaries find their wicked schemes thwarted by the heroic Pimpernel — Sir Percival Blakeney. In this thrilling sequel, Chauvelin devises a plot to eliminate the Pimpernel and his wife. 272pp. 5³⁄₁₆ x 8¼. 0-486-45464-9

AN ENCYCLOPEDIA OF BATTLES: Accounts of Over 1,560 Battles from 1479 B.C. to the Present, David Eggenberger. Essential details of every major battle in recorded history from the first battle of Megiddo in 1479 B.C. to Grenada in 1984. List of battle maps. 99 illustrations. 544pp. 6½ x 9¼. 0-486-24913-1

ENCYCLOPEDIA OF EMBROIDERY STITCHES, INCLUDING CREWEL, Marion Nichols. Precise explanations and instructions, clearly illustrated, on how to work chain, back, cross, knotted, woven stitches, and many more — 178 in all, including Cable Outline, Whipped Satin, and Eyelet Buttonhole. Over 1400 illustrations. 219pp. 8⅜ x 11¼. 0-486-22929-7

ENTER JEEVES: 15 Early Stories, P. G. Wodehouse. Splendid collection contains first 8 stories featuring Bertie Wooster, the deliciously dim aristocrat and Jeeves, his brainy, imperturbable manservant. Also, the complete Reggie Pepper (Bertie's prototype) series. 288pp. 5⅜ x 8½. 0-486-29717-9

ERIC SLOANE'S AMERICA: Paintings in Oil, Michael Wigley. With a Foreword by Mimi Sloane. Eric Sloane's evocative oils of America's landscape and material culture shimmer with immense historical and nostalgic appeal. This original hardcover collection gathers nearly a hundred of his finest paintings, with subjects ranging from New England to the American Southwest. 128pp. 10⅝ x 9. 0-486-46525-X

ETHAN FROME, Edith Wharton. Classic story of wasted lives, set against a bleak New England background. Superbly delineated characters in a hauntingly grim tale of thwarted love. Considered by many to be Wharton's masterpiece. 96pp. 5³⁄₁₆ x 8 ¼. 0-486-26690-7

THE EVERLASTING MAN, G. K. Chesterton. Chesterton's view of Christianity — as a blend of philosophy and mythology, satisfying intellect and spirit — applies to his brilliant book, which appeals to readers' heads as well as their hearts. 288pp. 5⅜ x 8½. 0-486-46036-3

THE FIELD AND FOREST HANDY BOOK, Daniel Beard. Written by a co-founder of the Boy Scouts, this appealing guide offers illustrated instructions for building kites, birdhouses, boats, igloos, and other fun projects, plus numerous helpful tips for campers. 448pp. 5³⁄₁₆ x 8¼. 0-486-46191-2

FINDING YOUR WAY WITHOUT MAP OR COMPASS, Harold Gatty. Useful, instructive manual shows would-be explorers, hikers, bikers, scouts, sailors, and survivalists how to find their way outdoors by observing animals, weather patterns, shifting sands, and other elements of nature. 288pp. 5⅜ x 8½. 0-486-40613-X

FIRST FRENCH READER: A Beginner's Dual-Language Book, Edited and Translated by Stanley Appelbaum. This anthology introduces 50 legendary writers — Voltaire, Balzac, Baudelaire, Proust, more — through passages from *The Red and the Black, Les Misérables, Madame Bovary,* and other classics. Original French text plus English translation on facing pages. 240pp. 5⅜ x 8½. 0-486-46178-5

FIRST GERMAN READER: A Beginner's Dual-Language Book, Edited by Harry Steinhauer. Specially chosen for their power to evoke German life and culture, these short, simple readings include poems, stories, essays, and anecdotes by Goethe, Hesse, Heine, Schiller, and others. 224pp. 5⅜ x 8½. 0-486-46179-3

FIRST SPANISH READER: A Beginner's Dual-Language Book, Angel Flores. Delightful stories, other material based on works of Don Juan Manuel, Luis Taboada, Ricardo Palma, other noted writers. Complete faithful English translations on facing pages. Exercises. 176pp. 5⅜ x 8½. 0-486-25810-6

Browse over 9,000 books at www.doverpublications.com